Colin Spencer

FEAST *for* HEALTH

A GOURMET GUIDE
TO GOOD FOOD

Illustrated by the author

Dorling Kindersley • London

A Jill Norman Book

First published in Great Britain in 1987
by Dorling Kindersley Limited,
9 Henrietta Street, London WC2 8PS

Jacket photograph of author by Barbara Machin

Typeset by
Wyvern Typesetting Ltd, Bristol
Printed by
Butler & Tanner, Frome, Somerset

British Library Cataloguing in Publication Data

Spencer, Colin
  Feast for health.
  1. Cookery (Natural
foods)
  I. Title
  641.5′637   TX741

ISBN 0–86318–220–8

Contents

PREFACE

Most people now understand roughly what the healthy diet is. In the affluent West, we eat too much fat, saturated fat in particular, too much sugar and salt and not enough dietary fibre. We should cut down by a third to a half on fat, sugar and salt and certainly double our intake of dietary fibre. But what does all this really mean? A third or a half of what? This book tells you in the most practical way by taking a week out of each season and giving recipes for every day, so that you can clearly see how the overall diet looks. What is more, *Feast for Health* does not go in for a spartan course of meals, it shows you that you can eat healthily and like a gourmet at the same time.

In a general fashion, the healthy diet means more fresh vegetables and fruit, more fish, less dairy produce and meat, more grains and pulses.

Meat and fowl[1] (and all factory farming) engender strong feelings in me. Meat tends to have a high percentage of saturated fat; the cheaper cuts obviously have more. So for this reason alone, meat eaters should watch the amount they consume and cut down by at least a half. Factory farming has now become big business and is heavily dependent on chemicals. There are no restrictions and no safeguards on the amount of drugs the farmer may give to his livestock. Antibiotics are freely given, as animals in close quarters are vulnerable to diseases. Growth hormones are also given to add quick bulk which, because of the lack of exercise for the animal, ends up as fat instead of muscle. The high protein feed (often imported from Third World countries) thus produces a carcass high in saturated fat and with residues of chemical hormones (one now thankfully banned, DES, has been proved to be carcinogenic) and residues of antibiotics which will affect the consumer. There are some strains of salmonella bacteria that are now resistant to antibiotics. We know that the regular injection of antibiotics stops them being of therapeutic use. Hence there are now many more

---

[1] Not many people realize that ducks, geese and turkeys are all factory farmed now. Sadly, some game birds like partridge and quail are as well.

cases of salmonella poisoning and more people are dying from it. But it is the long-term risk of eating carcasses which have been treated with growth hormones which is most worrying.

In my view, there are also other reasons for not eating factory-farmed meat and poultry. The animals lead an unnaturally short life and are very often deformed by overcrowding in close stalls where they can rarely move more than a few inches throughout their life. This is inhumane. The protein feed taken from Third World countries deprives the population of much-needed food and helps to produce malnutrition and famine, stressing the difference between rich and poor. It strikes me as one of the most immoral and obscene facts of life today that a broiler chicken (the kind found on every supermarket shelf) has had a better nutritional feed than 60 percent of the people in the world today.

Factory-farmed products therefore cannot be in any way good for us and can very likely do harm. Too many people suffer from allergies and depression, from feeling under par, and more and more evidence tells us that this is quite likely to be due to the chemical cocktail.

In some ways, the story of the fowl at the moment is particularly worrying. Although red meat sales are declining, chicken sales are booming and, though I consider that this bland and flabby meat should be avoided for reasons of taste, there are now serious health hazards involved for people who eat factory-farmed chicken. Eight out of ten chickens carry the salmonella bacteria which, though it is killed by thorough cooking, is highly contagious at all stages before this. To cut up a raw chicken in the kitchen where there is other food nearby is now a most foolish act. How can we have reached a stage where manufacturers are selling to the public food which is toxic?

It seems superfluous then to add that there are no chicken or meat dishes in these pages. But there is fish and some game. Fish has mostly polyunsaturated fats and is rich in minerals and vitamins. Game too is very low in fat, high in protein and of unique flavour: a creature which forages for its own food will eat a diversity of vegetation, giving its flesh an intense flavour that factory-farmed animals lack.

The healthy diet then should be based simply and squarely on grains, pulses, fruits and vegetables, with fish perhaps three times a week and game, when it is in season, perhaps once a week.

Out of these ingredients, you can create a stylish and delicious diet. One of the most fascinating facts is that the healthy diet (as outlined above) has become the present gourmet diet, although contemporary gourmets, it must be said, are not yet alive to the dangers and ugliness of factory farming, so they would include, alas, some portion of meat in this selection. Yet, nutritionally, meat is not necessary and, as I have explained, it can now also be a hazard to health.

INTRODUCTION

The problem in creating these weeks of healthy eating was how to make it practical and believable. I have imagined a family of four seated at home for dinner and perhaps two of those four at home in the day. So lunch, which is simple, is always for two and breakfast is merely a suggestion of a dish, for one or more. I have also imagined a dinner party on the Saturday evening for six to eight people and a brunch on the Sunday for ten to twelve people. That means a heavy weekend's entertaining and, it must be said, perhaps a little over-eating. Yet, when you divide the amount of food by the number of people, perhaps not.

But how could all this food be bought and cooked by one or two people? It would be constant activity, tireless work in the kitchen leading perhaps to boredom with eating at all. In this sense, the whole structure and details of the week are unrealistic. So what I have tried to do is give a blueprint, a kind of plan of what it might be to eat healthily and like a gourmet, knowing that no one is actually going to do this for the whole week. What you might do is to pick a day or two and follow those; see how the choice and amounts of food go and try your own ideas from that. If I had made the weeks realistic, the recipes would have been even simpler and the evening meal might have included only one dish followed by fruit and cheese. In an effort to make the book practical, I have also created the working person's week with simpler and quicker dishes which need little preparation and very occasionally use convenience foods.

On the subject of the book's practicality, I also came up against the thorny subject of 'leftovers'. Most food writers and recipe books try to avoid it but, in life, we all spend at least a third of our kitchen time creating dishes out of them. I personally am rather fond of leftovers. Spicy dishes often mature after being left. Once the blender has got at them, their whole character can change. In this book I have compromised. I have given recipes for fresh ingredients but some of the luncheon dishes follow on from the night before, in the sense that if there was something left over from a fish curry and mung dhal, it would make, with the addition of water, a pretty splendid soup. If there is not, there is a recipe for mung bean soup anyway but without the curry flavouring, in case the palate of the night before was so sated it now needed to be refreshed. Similarly, the falafels of dried pea could be made from blending and reducing the cabbage and pea soup. I found making new dishes out of leftovers was natural in winter and, to a lesser degree, in autumn, but not so much in spring and summer where, if any food was left over, it would probably be eaten cold, raided from the refrigerator.

TABOO FOODS

FATS

Milk, when used, is skimmed. Low fat curd cheese, fromage frais and quark are usually used instead of cream. The only other saturated fat I have used in the cooking is butter and it is used for flavour. I have never believed in substituting margarine, which tastes foul so will not help the flavour of the dish. I also believe there are too many additives in margarine for the consumer's comfort. If you cut down on other fats, then butter can be used in cooking. Avoid spreading it on toast or bread: use quark or a spread without fat. If you must use butter, spread it thinly.

The oils used are mainly olive oil, which is monosaturated, and, occasionally polyunsaturated oils like corn, groundnut and sunflower. The most delicious oils are walnut, hazelnut and sesame oil, the last being high in protein. Beware of coconut, palm and oils just labelled 'vegetable'. These will be made of oils that are high in saturated fats. Beware the hidden fats in so many manufactured foods which may be eaten as snacks.

SUGAR

I have seldom used sugar at all in this book. When a little sweetening is necessary, I have used honey. But do not be fooled that honey does not cause caries (dental decay); all sugars do. If you have young children, it is best never to introduce them to sweet flavours. But I have included honey because it is a more intricate compound than refined sugar. It does not contain sucrose, the sugar which does the most damage, for the bees have broken this substance down, but it does have large amounts of fructose (the sugar in fresh fruit), and among others, glucose.

SALT

Although sea salt appears in the recipes, it is up to the cook whether to use salt or not. The latest nutritional advice we have is that the case against salt is not utterly proven, that what hardens the arteries and helps to cause coronaries could be the balance between three salts, potassium, sodium and calcium. However, it is also agreed that we tend to eat far too much salt and that none should be added in the cooking. In the directions, I generally say to add salt at the last moment, after tasting and checking.

ON DIETARY FIBRE

Some people seem to think that fibre is what it says, some hempen material in food which must be like the indigestible outside of celery stalks. It is not, thank goodness, though celery contains it. There is certainly no need to eat tough celery stalks or anything else that is tough. Raspberries and blackberries, for example, are high in fibre. So are all root vegetables and fruit, like apples, pears, bananas and avocados.

Fibre is the substance in the cells of plants which the enzymes in our digestive tract cannot break down. It acts by wrapping around the toxic substances and bolstering them, so that they can be passed through the bowel. A diet without fibre allows the toxins in the food to pass into the rest of the body.

ORGANIC FOODS

If possible, buy naturally grown organic foods. They do taste a lot better; in fact, you will be astonished at the difference. You need then have no worries about pesticide residues in the vegetables. Plainly steamed, fresh vegetables which have been grown organically are a world apart from those clingfilm-wrapped on the supermarket shelf.

FREE-RANGE EGGS

Whenever possible, buy free-range eggs. There is a difference in flavour and a marginal difference in nutritional quality. But the most important reason for buying them is that the battery hen leads a brutish and cruel existence, beakless, featherless and deformed. It is an egg-laying machine overfed with protein and often suffering from diseases related to its unnatural confinement. If we all saw pictures of a battery hen beside the eggs in the supermarket, we would never buy them. Do help to put pressure on this cruel trade which contradicts flagrantly an EEC convention on the welfare of farm animals.

ON THE IMPERFECT PERSON

When writing instructions for each season, I was struck by the concept which I had of the perfect person – the ideal housekeeper, woman or man, who did everything brilliantly. The one – you know them well – who bakes the bread, makes home-made muesli and yoghurt, has time to pickle onions, makes jams and jellies, freezes soft fruit, entertains with style and is also the most content and loving parent and spouse. I doubt whether such a person exists, although we may all swear that so-and-so actually is all that and more. In fact, I think we would all be more competent and serene if we dumped this image of the perfect person in the bin. What is more, I am sure that many people make themselves feel inferior and unwanted because they do not meet up with this image they carry around inside themselves.

The truth is that we probably have a go at being good as a cook, housekeeper, and provider and constantly have mishaps and make mistakes. We are, thank God, imperfect – all of us. And there is singularity in these imperfections which in cooking, quite often, makes the dish unique. So my message is, relax and have a bash at it. It doesn't matter much if there are failures. They too have their uses, for we learn more from a failure than a success. Relaxation about your task is important for another reason – health is as much to do with the mind as the body. If you worry about whether you are doing the right thing, eating the right food and get into a panic about failing, you will be doing your own health more harm than good.

SERVINGS

The portions for all weekday dinners are for four people. The Saturday dinner party is planned for six to eight and the Sunday brunch for ten to twelve. The working person's meals are planned for one, though generously.

These meals have been planned with no snacks in mind, for I consider the dishes in themselves to be completely sustaining.

WINTER

Introduction

In winter, we need to eat more, of carbohydrates in particular, which is why the meals in this section are somewhat heavier.

BREAKFAST

Whatever the season, I believe in starting the day with fresh fruit juice and, in the winter, the citrus fruits are at their best. If you feel you need a hot drink, try a mixture of honey and lemon juice and hot water – excellent.

Most of the breakfasts can be prepared in advance, sometimes the night before as in the porridge and marinated cereal. Bread can be baked over the weekend for the days ahead. Muesli can be mixed and stored in an airtight jar.

BREAD

Baking bread is made much easier with the sachets of micronized yeast which are now available. These can be added dry to the rest of the ingredients and need no warm water treatment before. The bread will also be quite happy with only one proving. Some people enjoy kneading, finding it therapeutic. I have always found it rather a chore and like to use a food processor with dough hooks.

As the recipes in this book show, you can add a lot to a loaf, improving it nutritionally. But a home-baked loaf made just with wholemeal flour has a lot more flavour than most bought loaves.

One of my favourite loaves is the herb loaf. You can change the herbs that go into the dough, add minced onion and garlic as well as herbs, or add grated carrot and milled nuts. Bread is endlessly fascinating once you begin to bake. The stuffed vegetable loaf is particularly splendid with its lattice-work top.

SOUPS

It may seem dull to have soup every day throughout the week, but home-made soup can be so delicious and, nutritionally, it gives with the bread all the sustenance you need on a cold day. The soups are varied; even though pulses are used in four of them, the flavours are different, as are the textures. Soups are also fairly easy to make, and can be left to simmer over a low heat until you feel like eating. For these reasons, in the winter months, you can hardly do better than soup for all the family.

A word on stocks. You can make vegetable stock fairly easily at home out of celery, onion and parsley stalks. Boil these together and let them simmer for half an hour. Allow to cool, blend, sieve, save the liquor and throw away the vegetable debris. Stocks, of course, can be made from the peelings of vegetables and often from the tough outside leaves. But if you haven't time to make stock, then buy pure vegetable stock cubes. Wholefood shops stock them. Avoid chicken and meat cubes for two reasons, (1) they make soups all taste the same and as if they have come out of a tin and (2) the cubes are made from those parts of carcasses that cannot be used for any other purpose and they are heavily tainted with additives.

GRAINS AND PULSES

I have put these two together because they should play a large part in the diet. Eaten together in the same meal, they make what is known as complementary protein. The classic example always given is baked beans on toast. But bean or lentil soups with wholemeal bread, which is the daily winter lunch, is also a perfect example of complementary protein. Put simply, this is where two foods act like the perfect jigsaw, fitting exactly together, supplying elements which the other food lacks and vice versa. The meal then comprises whole protein without needing to eat meat, chicken, fish or eggs.

Do experiment with different grains – I have tried throughout this book to use them all. And the pulse family is varied and large; aduki beans, for example, are a great Japanese standby, but not much used elsewhere. This is a pity, for this small, and prettily coloured bean is one of the highest in protein.

SALADS

Some raw food should be eaten once a day. It does not matter how or where. It could be in a sandwich or a side salad, or in a more substantial salad. The salads in the winter section are not recipes in themselves but merely indications of part of the main meal in the evening. There are now, in the winter, a greater variety of salad leaves available. Many new chicories and endives are being imported from France and Italy. They make colourful salads which are as tasty as they look.

If, on the other hand, you have only winter lettuce or Chinese leaves, the salad can be made more interesting with a dressing made from flavoured oil and vinegar. Add a little walnut, hazelnut or sesame oil to extra virgin olive oil; experiment with balsamic and fruit vinegars. Add crushed garlic, honey, paprika or mustard. For more interest, you can use fruit and nuts, but be cautious when adding nuts, as too many can overload a light side dish.

CHEESE AND FRESH FRUIT

The perfect way of finishing a meal if both are in peak condition. But too much cheese can bump up your saturated fat intake, so be circumspect. In the winter, we need to eat a little more fat anyway, and those delicious high fat cheeses like Roquefort, Brie and Dolcelatte are best enjoyed then. There are now more and more good low fat cheeses which can be eaten all the year round.

British cheeses made by small farms are as good and as individual as the French ones. Ask your cheese stockist to get these new British cheeses, like Swaledale, Yarg, Beenleigh Blue and Cotter (to name but a few). Some of these cheeses are low in fat too. Experiment. There is, for example, a wonderful matured Gouda which, knowing the young cheese, I would never have thought worth eating. It is low in fat and can be used, if you wish, like Parmesan, grated over pasta.

Monday

BREAKFAST

Fresh fruit juice

Porridge

Herb tea

LUNCH

Lentil and onion soup

Wholemeal bread

DINNER

Walnut and onion moulds in cabbage leaves

•

Fish, potato and mushroom curry

Saffron rice

Mung bean dhal

•

Chicory and orange salad

•

Cheese and fresh fruit

Porridge

8 oz (250 g) whole oats or oat groats
3 pints (1.8 litres) water
1 teaspoon sea salt

This porridge is made from the whole oat kernel, with all its flavour and nourishment.

Bring the water to the boil. Pour over the oats in a large oven dish. Add the salt and place in a very low oven, 275°F/140°C/gas 1, overnight. In the morning, you should have a creamy porridge to which you can add yoghurt, honey and dried fruit.

Note: All ovens are different – some low ovens may not cook the mixture enough and others might dry it out. Adjust the temperature accordingly. A Rayburn or Aga second oven is perfect for this method.

Lentil and Onion Soup

3 tablespoons olive oil
good pinch each of ground oregano, rosemary and sage
3 cloves of garlic, crushed
2–3 medium onions, sliced finely
5 oz (150 g) orange lentils, soaked for 1 hour
2½ pints (1.5 litres) vegetable stock or water
1 bay leaf
sea salt and freshly ground black pepper

FOR THE GARNISH
green tops of spring onions, chopped small
sprinkling of finely chopped parsley

Heat the oil in a pan and sweat the ground herbs and garlic for a moment. Then add the onions, lower the heat, and sweat these until soft. Add the drained lentils, stir and cook for a moment. Add the stock or water and bay leaf, bring to the boil and simmer for 40 minutes.

Season to taste and leave to cool. Blend to a smooth purée and then reheat gently. Sprinkle with the garnish before serving.

Wholemeal Bread

1 lb (500 g) wholemeal flour
1 teaspoon sea salt
2 tablespoons olive oil
1 tablespoon malt extract
1 tablespoon black treacle
1 sachet of micronized yeast
scant ½ pint (300 ml) warm water

Mix all the ingredients together and knead the dough for a good 6–8 minutes if using dough hooks – 10 minutes if kneading by hand.

If you are using a bread tin (1 lb/500 g size), grease it liberally, shape the dough and place it in. Cover with a cloth or clingfilm and leave in a warm place until it has filled the tin (about 1 hour). (If you are not using a bread tin, shape the dough into a round or oval, place it on a greased baking tray and cover with an upturned bowl.)

Bake the bread in a preheated oven, at 425°F/220°C/gas 7, for 45 minutes. When it is done it will sound hollow when tapped on the bottom.

Walnut and Onion Moulds in Cabbage Leaves

4–6 cabbage leaves
1 oz (25 g) butter
2 large onions, sliced
3 oz (75 g) walnuts, chopped
4 oz (125 g) curd cheese
2 eggs, beaten
sea salt and freshly ground black pepper

Blanch the cabbage leaves for 2 minutes, then drain by draping them over the sides of a colander. Butter 4 or 6 ramekin dishes.

Melt the butter in a pan and cook the sliced onions until soft and transparent. Do not let them brown. In a bowl mix the walnuts, curd cheese, cooked onions and eggs together. Taste and season.

Arrange the cabbage leaves in the ramekins so that they cover the bottoms and sides, leaving enough overhang for the tops. Fill with the mixture, allowing for each to rise a little in cooking. Fold the cabbage leaves over the tops and place the ramekins in a baking dish half filled with boiling water. Protect the tops with buttered paper and cook in a preheated oven, 400°F/200°C/gas 6, for 15 minutes.

Allow to rest for 5 minutes before unmoulding.

Fish, Potato and Mushroom Curry

3 tablespoons corn oil
3 cloves of garlic, crushed
1 onion, sliced
2 oz (50 g) fresh root ginger, peeled and sliced thinly
2 dried red chillies, broken up
½ teaspoon each of ground fenugreek and turmeric
½ teaspoon each of coriander, cumin, cardomom and mustard seeds
1½ lb (750 g) potatoes, peeled and diced
8 oz (250 g) mushrooms, sliced
2 pints (1.2 litres) water
sea salt, to taste
2 lb (1 kg) white fish (cod, hake, haddock), skinned, boned and
cut in chunks
1 oz (25 g) creamed coconut, grated

Heat the oil in a large pan. Add the garlic, onion, ginger root, chillies and spices. Cook for a few minutes before adding the potatoes and mushrooms. Add the water and a pinch of salt. Bring to the boil and simmer for 15 minutes before adding the fish. Stir and simmer for another 5 minutes. Taste to check the seasoning again, then add the coconut. Stir and simmer for 2 minutes.

Let the dish rest away from the heat for a further 5 minutes before serving.

Saffron Rice

pinch of sea salt
½ teaspoon saffron strands
6 oz (175 g) Patna rice

Boil 12 fl oz (350 ml) water in a saucepan with the salt and saffron. Add the rice, give it a stir, place the lid on the pan and simmer for 6 minutes or until the water is absorbed. When the rice is al dente, pour it into a colander and place in a warm oven, 350°F/180°C/gas 4 for another 3–5 minutes.

Fluff with a fork before turning into a serving dish.

Mung Bean Dhal

3 tablespoons corn oil
1 small piece of cassia
1 small piece of tamarind
1 teaspoon juniper berries, crushed roughly
5 oz (150 g) mung beans, soaked overnight
2 tablespoons garam masala
sea salt, to taste

Heat the oil in a pan. Add the cassia, tamarind and juniper berries, and cook for a moment. Add the drained mung beans and 1½ pints (850 ml) of water. Bring to the boil and simmer for 30 minutes, then add the garam masala and salt to taste.

Pour into an oven dish, remove the cassia and tamarind and cook in a preheated oven, 350°F/180°C/gas 4, for a further 30 minutes or until the liquid in the dhal has evaporated.

Chicory and Orange Salad

2–3 heads of chicory
2 oranges
1 tablespoon sesame oil
sea salt and freshly ground black pepper

Separate the leaves of the chicory and lay them out on a serving platter. Carefully peel the oranges, making sure all the pith is removed, separate into segments and reserve the juice. Lay the orange segments in the inside of the chicory leaves. Mix the orange juice with the oil and seasoning and dribble a little over each leaf.

Tuesday

BREAKFAST

Fresh fruit juice

High protein loaf

Curd cheese and honey

Herb tea

LUNCH

Mung bean soup

Wholemeal bread (page 22)

DINNER

Hot avocado soup

•

Onion tart

Baked potatoes

•

Cabbage and apple salad

•

Chocolate cream

High Protein Loaf

1 lb (500 g) wholemeal flour
1 teaspoon sea salt
2 tablespoons olive oil
1 tablespoon malt extract
1 tablespoon black treacle
1 tablespoon cracked wheat
1 tablespoon bran
1 tablespoon each of soya flour, wheatgerm, linseeds and
dried milk powder
sesame seeds, for sprinkling on top
scant ½ pint (300 ml) warm water
1 sachet of micronized yeast

Although this is a heavy loaf, it is delicious and makes a particularly good, crunchy toast for breakfast.

Mix all the ingredients except the sesame seeds together and knead the dough for a good 6–8 minutes if using dough hooks, 10 minutes if by hand.

If you are using a bread tin, grease it liberally and place the dough in it. Cover with a cloth or clingfilm and leave in a warm place until it has filled the tin. (If you are not using a bread tin, shape the dough into a round or oval and place on a greased baking tray covered with an upturned bowl.) This loaf will take all of 2 hours to rise and will probably only just double its bulk.

Sprinkle the top of the loaf liberally with sesame seeds and bake the bread in a preheated oven, 425°F/220°C/gas 7, for 45 minutes. If you tap it on the bottom it will sound hollow when done.

Mung Bean Soup

3 tablespoons olive oil
3 cloves of garlic, crushed
1 tablespoon garam masala
8 oz (250 g) carrots, diced
1 large sweet potato, peeled and diced
4 oz (125 g) mung beans, soaked overnight
2½ pints (1.5 litres) vegetable stock or water
sea salt and freshly ground black pepper

Heat the oil in a pan. Sweat the garlic and garam masala for a moment, then add the carrot, sweet potato and drained beans. Cook for 2–3 minutes over a low heat before adding the vegetable stock. Simmer for 30 minutes or until the beans are tender. Taste and season.

Half of this soup can be puréed if you wish, then returned so that there are whole beans in a thickish soup.

Note: If making this soup from leftovers of the mung bean dhal (*page 24*), 1½ cups of dhal to 3 cups of water will give enough soup for 4 people. There will be enough flavouring in the dhal for the soup, although it will, of course, be different in flavour and texture to this soup.

Hot Avocado Soup

1 oz (25 g) butter
2 lb (1 kg) small courgettes, chopped small
sea salt and freshly ground white pepper
2½ pints (1.5 litres) vegetable stock
2 ripe avocados

FOR THE GARNISH
2–3 green tops of spring onions, chopped small

Melt the butter in a pan and add the courgettes then season and cook for a few minutes before adding the vegetable stock. Bring to the boil and simmer for 20 minutes. Leave to cool, then blend to a thin purée. Add the flesh from the avocados and blend again. Reheat gently – the soup must not boil.

Add the garnish just before serving.

Onion Tart

FOR THE PASTRY
3 oz (75 g) wholemeal flour
3 oz (75 g) plain flour
3 oz (75 g) butter, iced and grated
pinch of sea salt
scant tablespoon iced water and lemon juice
1 egg white

FOR THE FILLING
1½ oz (45 g) butter
3–4 large onions, sliced
2 tablespoons green peppercorns
½ pint (300 ml) smetana or sour cream
1 egg yolk
1 oz (25 g) Gruyère, grated
pinch of sea salt
6 black olives, stoned

First make the pastry. Sift the flours, then sprinkle the bran back in. Add the butter and salt and combine until you have a good crumbly mixture, the consistency of dry breadcrumbs. Add just enough iced water and lemon juice to make a paste. Cover with clingfilm and refrigerate for 1 hour. Bring back to room temperature.

Butter a tart tin, 11 in (28 cm) × 1 in (2.5 cm), and line with the pastry. Fill with ceramic beans and bake blind in a preheated oven, for 10 minutes 425°F/220°C/gas 7. Remove the beans, paint the pastry with the egg white and bake again for a few minutes.

Meanwhile, melt the butter and add the sliced onions, cooking gently until soft. Take from the heat and add the peppercorns, smetana, egg yolk, Gruyère and salt. Stir thoroughly and pour into the tart. Slice the olives in half and place them in a pattern into the onion purée. Bake in a preheated oven, 400°F/200°C/gas 6, for 20 minutes or until just brown on top.

Cabbage and Apple Salad

1 small white cabbage, grated
2 cooking apples, grated
2 oz (50 g) hazelnuts, broken roughly
1 tablespoon walnut oil
2 tablespoons olive oil
½ teaspoon lemon juice
sea salt and freshly ground black pepper

Mix the cabbage, apples and nuts together thoroughly. Make the dressing, stir it into the salad and leave for 15 minutes before serving.

Chocolate Cream

5 fl oz (150 ml) double cream
1 packet tofu (morinaga)
4 oz (125 g) bitter dark chocolate, grated
2 tablespoons soft brown sugar

Blend the cream and drained tofu together. Stir in the grated chocolate. Pour into six individual ramekins and sprinkle with the sugar. Refrigerate overnight.

Wednesday

BREAKFAST

Fresh fruit juice

Muesli

Herb tea

LUNCH

Cabbage and pea soup

Wholemeal bread (page 22)

DINNER

Falafels of split pea with hot caper sauce

•

Cod steaks in orange sauce

Parsnips with walnuts

Potato purée

•

Radicchio leaf salad

•

Cheese and fresh fruit

Muesli

Mix 8 oz (250 g) each of jumbo oatflakes, barley, rye and wheat flakes together. Add 4 oz (125 g) of bran and then 2 oz (50 g) each of mixed milled nuts, chopped nuts, sunflower or pumpkin seeds, stabilized wheatgerm and 4 oz (125 g) each of raisins and dried apricots.

This mixture can be stored for a few months, though after that the dried fruit becomes too dry.

To this, on the day, can be added a mixture of fresh fruit, or you can soak a portion of muesli in fruit juice. Dried fruit can be soaked in fruit juice separately and then added to the muesli, or cooked and added when cool.

Yoghurt, milk, honey, fruit juice or fresh fruit can be added at the table.

Cabbage and Pea Soup

3 tablespoons olive oil
1 onion, sliced thinly
½ white or savoy cabbage, sliced thinly
4 oz (125 g) split peas, soaked overnight
2½ pints (1.5 litres) vegetable stock or water
sea salt and freshly ground black pepper
1 oz (25 g) butter

FOR THE GARNISH
sprinkling of chopped parsley

Heat the oil in a saucepan and sweat the onion and cabbage for a few minutes; then add the drained peas. Stir and add the stock or water, bring to the boil and simmer for 30 minutes. Taste and season. Leave to cool, then blend to a purée. If it is too thick, add a little more water. Reheat gently, stirring in the butter at the last moment. Just before serving, sprinkle over the parsley.

Falafels of Split Pea

These falafels are made from leftover cabbage and pea soup. The soup will be very liquid, so pour into an oven dish and put into a medium oven, 350°F/180°C/gas 4, for 45 minutes, so that the liquid evaporates.

Add enough gram or besan flour to the split pea mixture to make a paste – 1½ tablespoons perhaps. Make small balls or cakes and roll them in wholemeal breadcrumbs. Shallow-fry so that the falafels are brown and crisp on the outside.

Serve on a bed of lettuce leaves with the following sauce:

Hot Caper Sauce

1 teaspoon wasabi powder (*page 168*)
2 tablespoons capers
2 tablespoons finely chopped parsley
sea salt and freshly ground black pepper
¼ pint (150 ml) sour cream

Mix the wasabi powder with a little water in a bowl to make a thin paste, and leave for 15 minutes. Mix the capers, parsley and wasabi paste together with a little salt and pepper, and beat into the sour cream.

Cod Steaks in Orange Sauce

4–6 cod steaks, 1 in (2.5 cm) thick
olive oil
freshly ground black pepper

FOR THE SAUCE
zest of 2 oranges
1 oz (25 g) butter
juice of 4–5 oranges (blood oranges would be particularly good)
1 teaspoon kuzu flour (*page 168*), mixed with a little water
salt and freshly ground black pepper

Make the sauce first. Place the zest with the butter in a pan. Heat and add the juice. When it is simmering, stir in the kuzu flour mixture and continue simmering for a moment until the sauce thickens. Check the seasoning. Keep the sauce warm while you grill the cod steaks.

Paint both sides of the steaks with oil, grind some black pepper over them and place under a hot grill for 2–3 minutes. Turn them over and cook the other side. They should not need longer than 4–5 minutes altogether. If there is skin on the fish, remove it before serving. Put the steaks on a dish and pour the sauce around them.

Parsnips with Walnuts

1½ lb (750 g) parsnips
3 fl oz (90 ml) olive oil
sea salt and freshly ground black pepper
1½ oz (45 g) broken walnuts

Trim and peel the parsnips. Cut them into 4 in (10 cm) slices and boil in salted water for 2 to 3 minutes. Drain well. Pour the oil into a gratin dish and turn the parsnips out into the dish. Season generously and turn them over in the oil. Bake in a preheated oven at 400°F/200°C/gas 6 for 20 minutes. Sprinkle the walnuts over the top and continue to bake for another 10 minutes until they are brown and crisp.

Potato Purée

Boil 2 lb (1 kg) of peeled potatoes in plenty of lightly salted water. Drain, mash and add about 2 oz (50 g) butter and 3 fl oz (75 ml) of skimmed milk. Add plenty of freshly ground black pepper and turn into a bowl. The purée can be kept warm in a low oven for a few minutes.

Radicchio Leaf Salad

Make a salad of mixed red lettuces, chicories and endives. Toss with lemon and olive oil and add some garlic croûtons (*page 129*).

Thursday

BREAKFAST

Hot lemon and honey
Wholemeal toast with miso or tahini spread

LUNCH

Black bean and ginger soup
Wholemeal bread (page 22)

DINNER

Smoked haddock moulds

•

Millet pilaf with black beans and ginger
Vegetable casserole

•

Chinese leaf salad

•

Cheese and fresh fruit

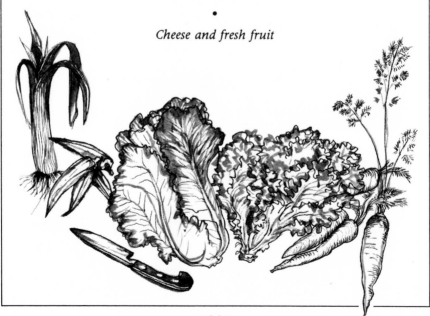

Black Bean and Ginger Soup

2 tablespoons sesame oil
4 oz (125 g) black beans, soaked overnight
2 oz (50 g) fresh root ginger, peeled and sliced very thinly
3 cloves of garlic, crushed
2½ pints (1.5 litres) vegetable stock (bought will do; *see page 169*)
1 carrot, julienne sliced
1 turnip, julienne sliced
2 oz (50 g) mushrooms, sliced
2 tablespoons soy sauce (shoyu – *see page 168*)
sea salt and freshly ground black pepper

FOR THE GARNISH
few spring onions, chopped

Heat the oil in a pan and add the beans, root ginger and garlic. Stir and cook gently for a few minutes, then add the vegetable stock. Bring to the boil, boil for 10 minutes and then simmer for 1 hour or until the beans are tender. Add the carrot and continue to simmer for 2 minutes; then add the turnip and mushrooms and cook for a further 2 minutes. Add the soy sauce, taste and check for seasoning.

Add the garnish before serving.

Smoked Haddock Moulds

1 oz (25 g) butter
1 finnan haddock
4 eggs, beaten
2 tablespoons smetana or sour cream
sea salt and freshly ground black pepper

Melt the butter in a pan over a gentle heat and place in the haddock. Cover the pan and let the fish steam in its own juice for 5 minutes. Cool, then skin and bone the fish. Place the flesh in a bowl with the juices and add the eggs, smetana and seasoning. Beat well.

Butter 4–5 ramekins and pour the mixture in. Place on a baking tin, pour in boiling water to come half way up the ramekins and protect the tops of the ramekins with buttered paper. Bake in a preheated oven, 400°F/200°C/gas 6, for 20 minutes.

Leave to cool, then unmould or serve in the ramekins.

Millet Pilaf with Black Beans and Ginger

This is a way of finishing up some of the black bean and ginger soup. Use 4 oz (125 g) of millet to about 12 fl oz (350 ml) of the soup and simmer the millet in it for 15 minutes, by which time it should have absorbed all the liquid.

If there is no leftover soup, follow the recipe below:

4 oz (125 g) millet
12 fl oz (350 ml) stock
1 oz (25 g) fresh root ginger, peeled and sliced very thinly
1½ oz (45 g) cooked black beans
salt and freshly ground black pepper
butter

Cook the millet in the stock with the ginger root for 15 minutes. Stir in the beans at the last minute. Season and add a knob of butter before serving.

Vegetable Casserole

2 tablespoons olive oil
1 tablespoon sesame oil
2 onions, sliced finely
3 cloves of garlic, crushed
2 green peppers, cored, seeded and sliced
1 teaspoon oregano
3–4 courgettes, trimmed and sliced
1 lb (500 g) Jerusalem artichokes, washed and chopped
1 lb (500 g) okra, trimmed
2 tablespoons light soy sauce
freshly ground black pepper
1½ pints (850 ml) vegetable stock

Heat the two oils in a pan and sweat the onions, garlic and peppers with the oregano. Add the courgettes, artichokes and okra, then the rest of the ingredients. Bring to the boil and simmer for 30 minutes. If it is too dry, add a little more stock. There should be a little liquid, but not too much.

Chinese Leaf Salad

6–7 Chinese leaves
8–10 kumquats
1 tablespoon thin honey
sea salt and freshly ground black pepper
1 oz (25 g) toasted, flaked almonds

Slice the Chinese leaves into pieces, ½ in (1 cm) wide by 3 in (7 cm) long, and blanch the stalk pieces in boiling water for a few minutes. Drain and place in a serving dish.

Slice the kumquats thinly, saving the juice. Mix the juice with the honey and seasoning. Toss the leaves in this, then sprinkle over the kumquats and almonds.

Friday

BREAKFAST

Fresh fruit juice

Marinated cereal

Herb tea

LUNCH

Leek and potato soup

Wholemeal bread (page 22)

DINNER

Herb Granary loaf (page 40)

Marinated white fish

•

Spinach mould with light blue cheese sauce

Couscous

•

Steamed celeriac

•

Fresh fruit

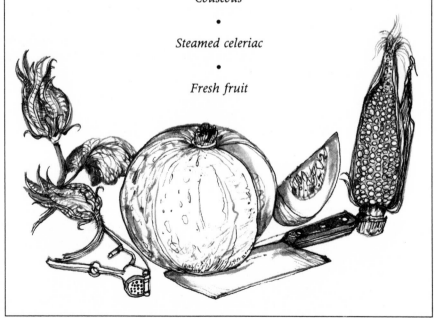

Marinated Cereal

2 tablespoons rolled oats
2 tablespoons bulgur wheat
1 tablespoon raisins
1 tablespoon dried apricots, chopped small
¼ pint (150 ml) fresh orange juice

Prepare this breakfast the night before. Put the dry ingredients together in a bowl, pour over the orange juice and leave in the refrigerator overnight.

Leek and Potato Soup

1 oz (25 g) butter
1 tablespoon olive oil
1½ lb (750 g) leeks, trimmed, cleaned and sliced
1 lb (500 g) potatoes, peeled and diced
2½ pints (1.5 litres) vegetable stock
sea salt and freshly ground black pepper

FOR THE GARNISH
1 tablespoon sour cream
sprinkling of chopped parsley

Melt the butter and heat the olive oil together in a pan. Add the leeks and potatoes and cook for 2 minutes. Add the stock, bring to the boil and simmer for 20 minutes. Taste and season. Leave to cool and blend to a thin purée.

Reheat gently and add the sour cream and parsley just before serving.

Herb Granary Loaf

8 oz (250 g) Granary flour
8 oz (250 g) strong white unbleached bread flour
1 teaspoon salt
2 tablespoons olive oil
1 sachet of micronized yeast
1 teaspoon each of celery seeds, dill seeds and crumbled sage
scant ½ pint (300 ml) warm water

Mix all the ingredients together and knead the dough for a good 6–8 minutes if using dough hooks – 10 minutes if by hand.

If you are using a bread tin, grease it liberally, shape and place the dough in it. Cover with a cloth or clingfilm and leave in a warm place until it has filled the tin. (If you are not using a bread tin, shape the dough and place it on a greased baking tray and cover with an upturned bowl.)

Bake the bread in a preheated oven, 425°F/220°C/gas 7, for 45 minutes. It is ready when it sounds hollow if tapped on the bottom.

Marinated White Fish

1 lb (500 g) monkfish, rock fish, dog fish or cat fish
juice and zest of 2 oranges and 1 lemon
1 tablespoon sea salt
1 tablespoon caster sugar
¼ pint (150 ml) white wine vinegar

Skin and bone the fish – or have your fishmonger do this for you. Mix all the other ingredients together. Slice the fish very thinly, place it in a shallow dish and pour the marinade over. Leave for 24 hours.

Serve the fish, without the marinade, fanned out over some salad leaves.

Spinach Mould with Light Blue Cheese Sauce

2 lb (1 kg) spinach
1 oz (25 g) butter
2 onions, sliced finely
2 eggs, beaten
½ pint (300 ml) single cream
pinch of freshly grated nutmeg
sea salt and freshly ground black pepper

FOR LIGHT BLUE CHEESE SAUCE
1 oz (25 g) butter
1 oz (25 g) plain flour
¾ pint (450 ml) skimmed milk
4 oz (125 g) Roquefort cheese mashed into a paste
freshly ground black pepper

Butter a 2½ pint (1.5 litre) soufflé mould or dish. Take out 5 or 6 of the largest spinach leaves – enough to line the mould – and blanch them in boiling water. Drain.

Melt the butter in a pan, add the onions and remaining spinach leaves, roughly torn, cover and cook over a low heat for about 8 minutes. If there is more than a couple of tablespoons of liquid left, reduce this by raising the heat. When cool, pour into a bowl and beat in the eggs, cream, nutmeg and seasoning.

Arrange the blanched spinach leaves over the bottom and sides of the mould dish, leaving enough overhang to cover the top. Pour in the mixture and fold the spinach leaves over. Place the mould in a baking tin, protecting the top with buttered paper. Fill the tin with boiling water to come half way up the sides of the dish and place in a preheated oven, 400°F/200°C/gas 6, for 40–45 minutes. Allow to rest for 5 minutes before unmoulding.

Serve with the light blue cheese sauce: make a roux with the butter and the flour. Add the milk slowly, then the Roquefort paste and black pepper to taste. Go on stirring until you have a smooth sauce. Serve hot.

Couscous

5 oz (150 g) couscous
juice and zest of 1 lemon
generous handful of parsley, chopped finely

Place the couscous in a colander, pour boiling water over it and leave for 20 minutes, raking the grains with your fingers 4 or 5 times so that lumps do not form.

Tip the couscous into a steamer with the lemon juice and zest. Steam over salted water for 20 minutes. Pour into a serving dish and stir in the parsley.

Steamed Celeriac Salad

2 or 3 small celeriac
sea salt and freshly ground black pepper

FOR THE SAUCE
1 egg yolk
juice and zest of 2 limes
1 tablespoon walnut oil
3 fl oz (90 ml) sour cream
sea salt and freshly ground black pepper

Peel the celeriac and cut into eighths. Slice each one of these pieces downwards again so that you have several strips. Season and steam for 15 minutes or until they are just tender but still crisp. Meanwhile, make the sauce in a bowl. Add the lime juice and zest to the egg yolk, then mix in the oil, sour cream and seasoning. While the celeriac is still warm, toss it in the sauce and serve.

Saturday

BREAKFAST

Hot lemon and honey

Dried fruit compote

Herb tea

LUNCH

Wholewheat spaghetti with mushroom sauce

DINNER PARTY

Avocado, papaya and smoked tofu salad

•

Simple pigeon casserole

Wild rice

Swiss chard purée

•

Mixed leaf salad

•

Apricot fool

•

Goat's cheese savoury

Dried Fruit Compote

2 oz (50 g) dried apricots, sliced
2 oz (50 g) mixed dried pears and apples, sliced
1 oz (25 g) dried figs, chopped
2 tablespoons raisins
½ pint (300 ml) apple juice

Prepare this breakfast the night before. Soak all the fruit in the apple juice overnight. In the morning, bring everything to the boil in a pan and simmer for 10 minutes. Leave to cool.

Wholewheat Spaghetti with Mushroom Sauce

Wholewheat or buckwheat spaghetti can now be purchased in wholefood shops and supermarkets in 8 oz (250 g) packets. Bring a large pan of salted water to the boil, and plunge 1 lb (500 g) spaghetti into it. Return to the boil, place a lid on the pan and turn the heat off. Leave for 5 minutes, then drain thoroughly, put into a large bowl and pour over the sauce.

MUSHROOM SAUCE
2 tablespoons olive oil
3 cloves of garlic, crushed
½ teaspoon ground asafoetida
½ teaspoon celery seeds
8 oz (250 g) mushrooms, sliced thinly and then chopped
4 large tomatoes, peeled and chopped
sea salt and freshly ground black pepper

Heat the olive oil in a pan and add the garlic, asafoetida and celery seeds. Sweat for 2 minutes, then add the mushrooms and tomatoes. Cook gently for 8 minutes. Taste and check for seasoning.

Avocado, Papaya and Smoked Tofu Salad

juice and zest of 2 limes
1 tablespoon sesame oil
sea salt and freshly ground black pepper
2 ripe avocados
2 ripe papayas
4 oz (125 g) smoked tofu
red lettuce leaves or radicchio
4 oz (125 g) haloumi cheese

In a wide, shallow dish, mix the juice and zest of the limes with the sesame oil and seasoning. Peel and stone the avocados and papaya. Slice them thinly and lay them in the dish. Slice the tofu thinly and add to the dish. Leave to marinate for 30 minutes.

Arrange the leaves on a serving platter or individual plates. Place on the pieces of avocado, tofu and papaya alternately in a fan pattern.

Dice the haloumi cheese into cubes and grill just before serving so that they are hot and sizzling. Scatter these over the salad.

Simple Pigeon Casserole

1 pigeon per person
2 tablespoons olive oil
2 large onions, sliced
5 cloves of garlic, chopped
1 teaspoon oregano
freshly ground black pepper
1 teaspoon celery salt
1½ lb (750 g) carrots, trimmed and sliced
sprig of rosemary
2 tablespoons shoyu sauce (*see page 168*)

FOR THE MARINADE
¼ pint (150 ml) red wine
3 fl oz (75 ml) brandy
1 teaspoon juniper berries, crushed

With kitchen scissors, cut the top of the birds away, that is, the two sides of the breast. Make the marinade and lay the breasts still on the bone, flesh side down, in it for 2 days. (Keep it in the refrigerator and forget about it.)

Meanwhile cook the rest of the pigeons. Heat the olive oil in a large casserole. Throw in the onions, garlic, oregano, pepper, celery salt, carrots and the pigeon carcasses. Tuck in the sprig of rosemary, cover with water, place a lid on the casserole, bring to the boil and simmer for 4–5 hours. Leave in the refrigerator for the 2 days.

Discard the carcasses and rosemary. (Give the meat to the cats, or use it in a pilaf.) Drain the pigeon breasts, reserving the marinade, and poach in the casserole with the stock and vegetables for 2 hours. Remove the skin and bones, leaving the flesh in the casserole. Add the marinade and shoyu, bring back to the boil and simmer for another 30 minutes. Serve hot.

Wild rice

Cover 8 oz (250 g) of wild rice with water in a pan and add a little salt. Bring to the boil and simmer for 10 minutes, then turn off the heat and let it rest for 1 hour. Add 2–3 peeled, chopped cloves of garlic and 1 finely sliced onion, and simmer for a further 15 minutes. Drain well and stir in some chopped parsley.

Swiss Chard Purée

Take 1½ lb (750 g) of this delicious vegetable and slice the stems from the leaf. Simmer the stems in a little salted water for 10 minutes. Tear the leaves into smaller scraps and add them to the saucepan. Simmer for another 5 minutes. Drain and place all the vegetable in a blender with 2 oz (50 g) of butter and seasoning, and blend to a purée. If stringy, sieve. Reheat gently.

Apricot Fool

4 oz (125 g) dried apricots, soaked overnight in apple juice
2 eggs, separated
3 fl oz (75 ml) apricot liqueur
1 pint (600 ml) smetana or sour cream
2 tablespoons toasted, flaked almonds

Put the soaked apricots in a pan with the apple juice. Bring to the boil and simmer for 5 minutes. Leave to cool and place in a liquidizer. Add the egg yolks, apricot liqueur and smetana, and blend to a thick purée. Pour into a mixing bowl. Whip the egg whites until stiff and fold into the mixture. Toast the flaked almonds for a few minutes in a warm oven or in a dry frying pan. Turn the fool out into a serving bowl and sprinkle with the flaked almonds.

Goat's Cheese Savoury

4–6 slices of herb granary loaf (*page 40*)
4 oz (125 g) goat's cheese
butter

Cut circles out of the pieces of herb bread a little bigger than the goat's cheese. Toast and then butter them. Place pieces of the cheese on the toast and grill until beginning to melt.

Sunday

BRUNCH

Fresh fruit juice

Cheese brioche

Stuffed pitta bread

Green pasta balls

Exotic fruit salad

Coffee

Bucks Fizz and mulled wine

SUPPER

Home-made baked beans on toast

Cheese Brioche

10 oz (300 g) strong white bread flour
4 oz (125 g) butter, diced
1 teaspoon salt
2 oz (50 g) Gruyère, grated
2 oz (50 g) Parmesan, grated
3 eggs, beaten
2 tablespoons milk
1 sachet micronized yeast

Combine the flour, butter, salt and cheeses in a bowl until the flour has absorbed the butter and cheese. Add the eggs, milk and yeast and knead for 5 minutes. As the dough is very sticky, it is best done with dough hooks in a food mixer. If doing it by hand, you will have to flour both your hands and the work surface. Leave to prove in a warm place for 1 hour.

When the dough has risen, put it in a buttered brioche or bread tin. Leave to prove again until the dough has risen to the top of the tin (about 15–20 minutes). Bake in a preheated oven, 375°F/190°C/gas 5, for 20–25 minutes. Turn out onto a wire rack to cool.

Stuffed Pitta Bread

2 onions, chopped
2 green chillies, seeded and chopped
corn oil
8 oz (250 g) cooked haricot beans
4 oz (125 g) cottage cheese
4 oz (125 g) cooked potato, diced
sea salt and freshly ground black pepper
½ teaspoon ground cumin
5–6 pitta bread

Cook the chopped onions and chillies in a little corn oil until soft. Mash the beans lightly in a mixing bowl, and add the cottage cheese and potato. Stir in the onion and chillies, season with salt, pepper and cumin and mix thoroughly. Stuff the halved pittas with the bean mixture. Serve warm.

Green Pasta Balls

4 oz (125 g) dried green tagliatelle
1 lb (500 g) spinach leaves, washed and well drained
4 oz (125 g) ricotta
2 oz (50 g) Gruyère, grated
2 oz (50 g) Parmesan, grated
pinch of nutmeg
sea salt and freshly ground black pepper
2 eggs
wholemeal breadcrumbs, for coating

Cook the green tagliatelle in plenty of boiling salted water until soft. Drain well. Cook the spinach leaves in a saucepan, without added water, over low heat until they have reduced to a third of their original bulk. Drain well. Combine the pasta and spinach and put in a blender. Reduce to a rough purée.

Add all the rest of the ingredients with the exception of 1 of the eggs and the breadcrumbs. Mix well. Place the mixture in a bowl and refrigerate briefly. Beat the remaining egg.

Roll the mixture into balls. Dip into the beaten egg and then coat with breadcrumbs. Refrigerate again before shallow- or deep-frying. Serve warm.

Exotic Fruit Salad

In the winter, there are so many imported fruits from the Far East and equatorial countries that it is possible to make uncommonly good fruit salads. It looks exciting if the colours are almost luridly bright, like a Tahitian painting by Gauguin.

Fruits to choose from are mango, papaya, lychee, guava, passion fruit, star apple, granadilla, pomegranate, pineapple and tamarillo. Peel and stone the fruits as necessary then they can all be sliced and tossed together, needing no added sugar. They could, if you wish, have a little eau-de-vie added to them or a fruit liqueur, but to my mind this hides the pure freshness of the fruit itself. These mixtures are so good, they are best au naturel.

Home-made Baked Beans

8 oz (250 g) small haricot beans or navy beans,
soaked overnight and drained
2 oz (50 g) butter
14 oz (395 g) can of tomatoes
3 tablespoons tomato purée
1 tablespoon raw cane sugar
sea salt and freshly ground black pepper

Combine all the ingredients, except the seasoning, in an earthenware crock or marmite (or, if cooking on top of the stove, in a saucepan). Bring to the boil and let it simmer. Add enough water to cover the beans by about 1 in (2.5 cm). Cover tightly with a lid or foil. Cook in a low oven, at 275°F/140°C/gas 1, for 5–6 hours. Inspect after 4 hours and add a little salt and pepper.

Alternatively, if cooking in a saucepan, simmer over a very low heat for 2 hours. Inspect every 20 minutes or so to make sure there is enough liquid and that the beans are not sticking.

A WORKING PERSON'S GUIDE TO WINTER

Start the day with fresh fruit juice and wholemeal toast with Vecon or honey. Or, the night before, prepare a small bowl of marinated cereal (*page 39, page 65* or *page 142*).

Lunch is a problem for many working people because business lunches tend to be rich and boozy. Avoid that kind of food, although you need not swing as far as Perrier water and a salad. Fortunately, there are now more wholefood restaurants around which do good soups. If you have to live within a tight budget, make a soup at home over the weekend and take it with you in a thermos. Or have one of the salads in this book as a sandwich in wholemeal bread.

Wholefood shops also sell excellent miso and seaweed soups, which can be enjoyed as they are or used as the basis for another soup, like a rich stock. They are high in food value.

The day for a working person can be often a lean time, so a well balanced meal ought to be consumed each evening. This can be difficult sometimes if you are tired, so I have tried to think up meals which are nutritious and yet easy to put together. There are now on sale excellent ready-made vegetarian meals – try these and find out the ones you like. However, pasta is perhaps one of the easiest dishes to make at home and wholewheat or buckwheat pasta can be bought easily.

Fish is quick and easy to cook. Cod steaks can be grilled briefly with a little oil or butter. Mackerel and herrings (get the fishmonger to gut them) can also be grilled without any added oil. Both are excellent in the winter with mustard or horseradish sauce. Cook some rice to go with them and chop up a few vegetables, like celery, fennel, mushroom, grated carrots or turnips, and add them to the rice in the last 2 minutes of cooking to cook them briefly.

Baked potatoes need an hour in the oven but they can be stuffed with low fat cheeses and chopped vegetables. They are also delicious of course with just a little butter or low fat sour cream, like Greek yoghurt, smetana, or fromage frais, mixed with a few chopped fresh herbs.

In these sections for the working person, I have used those convenience foods that I believe to be nutritionally good value and which are as free from additives as one should reasonably expect. Please though, as a matter of course, check all labels. All recipes are for one but are generous servings, so many would be enough for two.

Dinner

MONDAY

Wholewheat spaghetti with quick mushroom and tomato sauce
Cabbage and bean salad
Fruit and cheese

TUESDAY

Fish stew
Potato purée
Fruit and cheese

WEDNESDAY

Quick spinach and bean tart
Turnips with parsley and breadcrumbs
Fruit and cheese

THURSDAY

Smoked haddock pilaf
Green lentil dhal
Fruit and cheese

FRIDAY

Vegetable pie
Grapefruit, chicory and walnut salad
Cheese

MONDAY

Quick Mushroom and Tomato Sauce

1 small can of tomatoes
2 tablespoons olive oil
2 cloves of garlic, crushed
4 oz (125 g) mushrooms, sliced
sea salt and freshly ground black pepper
1 tablespoon tomato purée
2 tablespoons freshly grated Parmesan

Drain the tomatoes and chop them coarsely. Heat the oil in a pan, add the garlic and throw in the mushrooms. Cook for a few minutes. Add the tomatoes and cook for another 2 minutes. Lightly season, then stir in the tomato purée.

Cook some spaghetti (about 4 oz/125 g) and drain well. Pour the sauce over it and sprinkle over the Parmesan.

Cabbage and Bean Salad

14 oz (395 g) can of flageolet beans
½ small white cabbage, grated
1 small onion, peeled and grated
juice and zest of 1 lemon
3 tablespoons olive oil
sea salt and freshly ground black pepper

Drain the beans of all liquid and mix thoroughly with all the remaining ingredients.

Fish Stew

8 oz (250 g) cod steak, or other white fish
1 pint (600 ml) unpeeled prawns
2 tablespoons plain flour
2 tablespoons olive oil
1 large parsnip, diced
1 onion, sliced
1 small can of tomatoes
1 small packet of frozen broad beans
sea salt and freshly ground black pepper

Skin, bone and roughly chop the fish. Peel the prawns. Roll the fish pieces in the flour.

Heat the oil in a saucepan, add the fish and prawns, cook for a moment, then add the parsnip and onion. Cover the ingredients with water, bring to the boil and simmer for 10 minutes.

Drain the tomatoes and add to the pan with the beans. Season to taste, bring gently back to the boil and simmer for another 5 minutes.
Note: For a spiced fish stew, add some of the spices given for Monday's fish curry (*see page 23*).

Potato Purée

1 lb (500 g) potatoes, peeled and diced
2 tablespoons Greek yoghurt or fromage frais
3 tablespoons finely chopped parsley
sea salt and freshly ground black pepper

Cook the potatoes until tender. Drain well, add the other ingredients and mash to a thick purée.

Quick Spinach and Bean Tart

8 oz (250 g) frozen wholemeal puff pastry, thawed
8 oz (250 g) can of black-eyed beans
1 onion, sliced finely
½ oz (15 g) butter
½ oz (15 g) plain flour
¼ pint (150 ml) skimmed milk
2 oz (50 g) mature Cheddar, grated
1 small packet of frozen spinach, thawed
sea salt and freshly ground black pepper

Roll out the pastry and line an 8 in (20 cm) tart tin. Drain the beans, mix with the sliced onion, and spread over the pastry base.

Make a roux with the butter and flour. Add the milk, cheese and seasoning and cook until you have a smooth sauce. Mix the thawed spinach into the sauce and pour over the beans.

Bake the tart in a preheated oven, 400°F/200°C/gas 6, for 30 minutes.
Note: Start the baked potatoes first at the top of the oven. When you put the tart in, move the potatoes down to the centre with the tart above.

Turnips with Parsley and Breadcrumbs

1½ lb (750 g) small turnips
3 cloves garlic, chopped
3 tablespoons olive oil
generous handful of parsley, finely chopped
sea salt and freshly ground black pepper
1 oz (30 g) toasted breadcrumbs

Trim the turnips but do not peel them. Cut them into quarters and boil briefly in salted water – about 3 minutes. Drain well. Heat the olive oil in a pan, add the garlic and fry the turnips until they are crisp and brown. Stir in the parsley and seasoning. Then sprinkle the breadcrumbs over the top. Place under a hot grill until the top is crisp.

THURSDAY

Smoked Haddock Pilaf

4 oz (125 g) buckwheat
1 oz (25 g) butter
8 oz (250 g) courgettes, diced finely
1 onion, sliced
1 large finnan haddock
sea salt and freshly ground black pepper

Pour ½ pint (300 ml) of boiling water over the buckwheat in a pan and simmer for 10 minutes. Melt the butter in another pan, and throw in the courgettes and onion. Lay the haddock, skin side up, over the vegetables. Simmer for 10 minutes.

Drain the buckwheat well and place in an oven dish in a warm oven, 180°F/350°C/gas 4. Skin, bone and flake the smoked haddock, add to the vegetables and stir into the buckwheat. Season to taste.

Green Lentil Dhal

3 oz (75 g) green lentils
1 oz (25 g) root ginger, peeled and sliced finely
2 tablespoons corn oil
1 tablespoon garam masala
sea salt and freshly ground black pepper

Soak the lentils in the morning; drain them in the evening. Cover with fresh water in a pan, add the ginger root and simmer for 20 minutes. Drain and stir in the oil, garam masala and seasoning.

Vegetable Pie

8 oz (250 g) frozen wholemeal shortcrust pastry, thawed
8 oz (250 g) broccoli, sliced
8 oz (250 g) baby carrots, diced
8 oz (250 g) can of chick peas
2 tablespoons soy sauce
3 tablespoons water
½ teaspoon cornflour
freshly ground black pepper

Roll out two-thirds of the pastry to fit a small pie dish. Cook the broccoli and carrots until tender and drain well. Drain the chick peas. Mix everything together in a bowl.

Combine the soy sauce and water in a small pan, heat, and when simmering, add the cornflour to thicken slightly. Pour over the vegetables in the bowl. Add a little pepper; it should have enough salt. Fill the pastry case.

Roll out the remaining third of pastry for the top and fit over the pie dish, sealing the edges. Bake in a preheated oven, 400°F/200°C/gas 6, for 40 minutes.

Grapefruit, Chicory and Walnut Salad

1 pink grapefruit
2 heads of chicory
2 oz (50 g) broken walnuts
1 tablespoon walnut oil
2 tablespoons Greek yoghurt
sea salt and freshly ground black pepper

Peel the grapefruit, making sure all the pith is removed. (Save the juice and drink it.) Separate the segments. Separate the chicory leaves and place in a serving bowl. Pile the grapefruit segments on top of the leaves and scatter the broken walnuts over them. Mix the walnut oil, yoghurt and seasoning together and dribble over the salad.

SPRING

Introduction

As the weather becomes warmer, we not only eat less, we eat lighter food. It is not necessary to eat a large breakfast or stoke up on carbohydrates to keep warm. So the breakfasts indicated here are refreshing and nutritious without overloading the stomach.

I have given a recipe for marinated cereal in each season because I personally think it the best breakfast of all. The spring recipe is delicious and easily digestible and you can ring the changes with the ingredients. It has sunflower and other seeds sprinkled over it, and we too easily forget how seeds are powerhouses of energy. Imagine what a seed would do if germinated and you can begin to understand the condensed nutrition in this minute object.

Salads appear for lunch as they are quick to prepare and offer plenty of variety now that the fresh vegetables are appearing. Scatter a salad with a little fruit, nuts or cooked pasta, and eat a slice of wholemeal bread with it. If you find salads too boring, make a sandwich with them, spreading the bread with tahini, miso, Vecon or a low fat cheese. I especially like the crunch of raw vegetables combined with soft but tasty new bread, with a strong spread to enliven the taste sensation further. The only aspect to keep a cautious eye upon is the amount of fat which may creep into a meal like this, always remembering that some fat is necessary. Too much olive oil in the salad, or a mayonnaise, plus butter in the sandwich, if taken as a regular daily amount may be too much altogether. Leave butter out of the sandwich or watch the fat intake at supper.

Monday

BREAKFAST

Marinated cereal

Herb tea

LUNCH

Greek salad

Wholemeal pitta bread

DINNER

Haricot bean soup

•

Stir-fried spring vegetables with smoked tofu

Millet pilaf

•

Cheese and fresh fruit

Marinated Cereal

2 tablespoons rolled oats
2 tablespoons bulgur wheat
1 teaspoon sunflower seeds
1 teaspoon pumpkin seeds
¼ pint (150 ml) fresh apple juice (*page 142*)

Prepare this breakfast the night before. Put the oats and bulgur wheat in a bowl, scatter the seeds on top and pour over the apple juice. Leave in the refrigerator overnight.

Greek Salad

½ cos lettuce
2 large tomatoes, sliced thickly
½ cucumber, sliced thickly
1 onion peeled and sliced finely
10 black olives, stoned
4 oz (250 g) feta cheese, broken and crumbled
½ teaspoon oregano
sea salt and freshly ground black pepper
1 tablespoon lemon juice
3 tablespoons olive oil

Separate the leaves of the cos lettuce and lay them out in a bowl. Mix all the vegetables and feta cheese together and pile on top of the lettuce. Mix the oregano, seasoning, lemon juice and olive oil together and dribble over the salad before serving.

Haricot Bean Soup

2 tablespoons olive oil
3 cloves of garlic, crushed
1 onion, sliced thinly
1 teaspoon each of sage, rosemary and celery salt
2–3 carrots, diced
2–3 small turnips, diced
2–3 sticks of celery, chopped
2 medium potatoes, chopped
4 oz (125 g) haricot beans, soaked overnight
sea salt and freshly ground black pepper

Heat the oil in a pan. Throw in the garlic, onion and herbs. Cook for a moment or two, then add all the chopped vegetables. Continue to cook for a few more minutes before adding the drained beans. Pour in 2½ pints (1.5 litres) of water, bring to the boil, boil hard for 10 minutes, then simmer for 1 hour or until the beans are done.

Pour half of the soup into a blender and reduce to a purée. Pour back into the rest of the soup and check the seasoning. Reheat gently.

Stir-fried Spring Vegetables with Smoked Tofu

1 lb (500 g) broccoli
1 tablespoon sesame oil
1 lb (500 g) french beans, trimmed and sliced
2 small celeriac, peeled and sliced
4 oz (125 g) smoked tofu, diced
1 tablespoon light soy sauce
1 tablespoon dry sherry
1 bunch watercress, destalked and broken into sprigs
1 tablespoon toasted sesame seeds

Slice the florets from the broccoli stalks. Peel the stalks and slice them thinly. Toast the sesame seeds in a small pan over high heat. Keep shaking the pan so they don't stick and remove when the seeds change colour.

Heat the oil in a wok over high heat and add the broccoli, beans and celeriac. Stir-fry for 2 minutes, then add the tofu. Stir-fry for another 2 minutes, then add the soy sauce and sherry. Stir-fry for 1 minute. Throw in the watercress, and sprinkle with the sesame seeds before serving.

Millet Pilaf

2 tablespoons olive oil
2 onions, sliced finely
2 cloves of garlic, crushed
5 oz (150 g) millet
sea salt and freshly ground black pepper

Heat the oil in a pan and cook the onions and garlic gently until soft. Add the millet and seasoning, give it a stir and cover with enough boiling water to come ½ in (1 cm) above the millet. Gently simmer over a very low heat for 15 minutes.

Remove the pan from the heat and leave to rest for another 15 minutes before serving.

Tuesday

BREAKFAST

Stewed rhubarb

Yoghurt

Herb tea

LUNCH

Apple and celery salad

Wholemeal bread (page 22)

DINNER

Almond and leek soup

•

Seafood risotto

•

Green salad

•

Fresh fruit

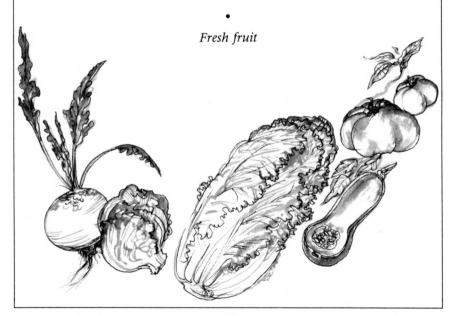

Stewed Rhubarb

Pick or buy rhubarb when it is young and pink: it is still astringent and will need honey to sweeten it a little. It can also be flavoured with ginger or angelica. Trim and slice the stalks into chunks. Place in a pan with the honey and let it soften. Once it has reached boiling point, it is done. Never add water.

Rhubarb is high in oxalic acid like spinach and sorrel. It is marvellous for cleaning saucepans.

Apple and Celery Salad

2 oz (50 g) mixed nuts, broken and ground
1 tablespoon sunflower seeds
2 dessert apples, sliced
1 head of celery, chopped
1 small onion, sliced thinly
1 tablespoon tahini
1 tablespoon lemon juice
3 tablespoons olive oil
sea salt and freshly ground black pepper
lettuce leaves, for serving

Combine all the ingredients and serve on the lettuce leaves.

Almond and Leek Soup

6 oz (175 g) almonds
1 oz (25 g) butter
1 lb (500 g) leeks, trimmed, cleaned and sliced
1 pint (600 ml) vegetable stock
1 pint (600 ml) skimmed milk
sea salt and freshly ground black pepper

Put the almonds in a liquidizer and crush them finely. Melt the butter in a pan and add the leeks; cook for a moment or two, then add the stock, crushed almonds and seasoning. Bring to the boil and simmer for 15 minutes. Leave to cool and then blend again.

Reheat, adding the milk. Taste and check the seasoning.

Seafood Risotto

1 oz (25 g) butter
2 tablespoons olive oil
1 onion, sliced
1 green pepper, cored, seeded and sliced
1 red pepper, cored, seeded and sliced
8 oz (250 g) white fish (cod, hake, huss, haddock, coley or whiting)
4 oz (125 g) prawns, shelled
4 scallops
sea salt and freshly ground black pepper
6 oz (175 g) Patna rice
½ teaspoon saffron threads
¼ pint (150 ml) dry white wine
1 bunch spring onions, chopped finely

Melt the butter and the oil in a large casserole. Throw in the onion and peppers and cook over a low heat for 15 minutes.

Bone and skin the white fish with care, then slice it. Detach the corals from the scallops and slice the white part in half. Add the fish to the casserole with the prawns and scallops. Stir and season before adding the rice, saffron, wine and enough water to cover the rice. Place a lid on the casserole and bake in a preheated oven, 375°F/190°C/gas 5, for 40 minutes.

Before serving, stir in the spring onions.

Wednesday

BREAKFAST

Fresh grapefruit

Herb tea

LUNCH

Bean and nut salad

Wholemeal bread (page 22)

DINNER

Moules marinière

•

Buckwheat and carrot croquettes

Baked potatoes

Stir-fried courgettes

•

Fresh fruit and cheese

Bean and Nut Salad

2 oz (50 g) cooked red kidney beans
2 oz (50 g) ground walnuts
1 small celeriac, grated
2 carrots, grated
2 potatoes, cooked and diced
2 tablespoons yoghurt
1 tablespoon lemon juice
sea salt and freshly ground black pepper

Combine all the ingredients together and toss thoroughly. Eat with a crisp lettuce and a slice of wholemeal bread.

Moules Marinière

3 quarts (3.6 litres) mussels
1 oz (25 g) butter
2 tablespoons olive oil
2 onions, sliced finely
1 clove of garlic, crushed
½ pint (300 ml) dry white wine
½ pint (300 ml) water
handful of parsley, chopped finely
sea salt and freshly ground black pepper

It is best, rather than scrubbing the mussels with a brush, to scrape them clean with a knife. This also cuts off the beard which protrudes from the shell. Discard any which remain open after being tapped sharply.

Heat the butter and oil in a large pan and add the onions and garlic. Stir for a minute or two, then throw in the mussels and cook them over a low heat for a minute or two, then add the wine and water. Cover and simmer for 5 minutes. Discard any mussels which remain shut. Throw in the parsley and a little seasoning, stir and serve.

Buckwheat and Carrot Croquettes

3 oz (75 g) buckwheat
1 lb (500 g) carrots
2 cloves of garlic, crushed
1 teaspoon ground sage
1 teaspoon celery seeds
1 tablespoon peanut butter
1 egg
sea salt and freshly ground black pepper
wholemeal breadcrumbs, for coating
oil, for frying

Put the buckwheat in a pan and cover with water. Bring to the boil and simmer for 10 minutes. Drain well. Meanwhile, cook the carrots until tender. Drain and blend with the garlic, sage and celery seeds.

Pour into a mixing bowl and add the buckwheat, peanut butter, egg and seasoning. Fashion into cake shapes, roll in the breadcrumbs and shallow-fry until crisp and brown.

Stir-fried Courgettes

1½ lb (750 g) small courgettes
½ bunch of spring onions
1 tablespoon sesame oil
1 tablespoon soy sauce (shoyu *see page 168*)

Trim the courgettes and slice them into thin strips 3–4 in (7–10 cm) long. Trim the spring onions and cut to about the same length as the courgettes. Heat the oil in a wok over high heat and throw in the courgettes. Move them around for 2 minutes, then add the spring onion. Cook for another minute, add the shoyu and cook for a further minute before serving.

Thursday

BREAKFAST

Wholemeal toast

Curd cheese and Vecon

Herb tea

LUNCH

Mixed bean salad

Wholemeal bread (page 22)

DINNER

Smoked eel pâté

•

Cabbage rolls

New potatoes

•

Apricot tofu

Mixed Bean Salad

2 oz (50 g) red kidney beans, soaked overnight
2 oz (50 g) black beans, soaked overnight
2 oz (50 g) soya beans, soaked overnight
1 tablespoon walnut oil
2 tablespoons olive oil
1 tablespoon lemon juice
sea salt and freshly ground black pepper
1 onion, sliced thinly
2 cloves of garlic, crushed
1 green pepper, cored, seeded and sliced
1 red pepper, cored, seeded and sliced

Cook all the beans together by boiling them in fresh water for 1½ hours. (Remember to boil the beans hard for the first 10 minutes.) Drain and cool.

Make a vinaigrette with the oils, lemon juice and seasoning. Mix all the vegetables together with the vinaigrette, then add the beans and toss thoroughly.

Eat with lettuce and wholemeal bread.

Smoked Eel Pâté

8 oz (250 g) smoked eel
juice and zest of 1 lemon
4 oz (125 g) curd cheese
4 tablespoons finely chopped chives
OR
5 oz (150 g) cottage cheese with chives
sea salt and freshly ground black pepper

FOR THE GARNISH
few capers and a lemon twist

Place the smoked eel in a blender with the rest of the ingredients and blend to a stiff purée. Transfer to a serving dish and garnish with a few capers and a twist of lemon.

Cabbage Rolls

leaves from 1 large savoy cabbage
8 oz (250 g) spinach leaves
2 onions, sliced thinly
1 teaspoon ground sage
4 oz (125 g) Patna rice
2 oz (50 g) Parmesan, grated finely
sea salt and freshly ground black pepper

Separate the cabbage leaves, blanch them in boiling water and leave for 5 minutes. Drain. Wash the spinach, drain well and cook with the onions and the sage over a low heat until the spinach is tender. Raise the heat to evaporate any moisture. Tip into a mixing bowl and chop the leaves into small pieces. Add the uncooked Patna rice and the Parmesan. Mix thoroughly and season.

Put about a tablespoon of the mixture on each cabbage leaf and roll up fairly loosely. Allow room for the rice to expand. Line the bottom of the pan with cabbage leaves then place the rolls on them, wedging them in against each other. Pour over enough water to cover them to half their level. Bring to the boil and simmer for 20 minutes.

Let the rolls cool in the water, which makes excellent stock, then take them out and drain. Reheat in a low oven, 325°F/160°C/gas 3, protected by buttered paper. They are also excellent cold.

Apricot Tofu

4 oz (125 g) dried apricots, soaked overnight
3 fl oz (90 ml) apricot liqueur
1 packet tofu (morinaga)
1 tablespoon honey

Simmer the apricots until they are soft, then reduce the liquor to nothing by raising the heat. Open the packet of tofu and drain. Place in the blender with the apricots and remaining ingredients and blend until smooth.

Friday

BREAKFAST

Fresh grapefruit

Herb tea

LUNCH

Tabbouleh

Wholemeal bread (page 22)

DINNER

Nut and mushroom pâté

•

Fish pie

Braised fennel

•

Fresh fruit

Tabbouleh

4 oz (125 g) bulgur wheat
juice and zest of 1 lemon
5 tablespoons olive oil
generous handful of mint, chopped finely
generous handful of parsley, chopped finely
4 tomatoes, chopped
1 bunch of spring onions, chopped finely
sea salt and freshly ground black pepper

Put the bulgur wheat in a bowl and pour over enough boiling water to cover. Leave for 30 minutes. Drain any excess water away – though the bulgur wheat should have absorbed all the moisture. Add all the other ingredients and toss well.

Nut and Mushroom Pâté

2 tablespoons olive oil
1 lb (500 g) mushrooms, sliced finely
2 onions, chopped
2 cloves of garlic, crushed
4 oz (125 g) walnuts, roughly crushed
2 eggs, hard-boiled and mashed finely
sea salt and freshly ground black pepper

FOR THE GARNISH
watercress

Heat the oil and cook the mushrooms, onions and garlic until soft. Place in a blender and liquidize to a rough purée. Pour into a bowl and mix in the rest of the ingredients. Press down into a dish and refrigerate for a few hours before serving.

Garnish with watercress and eat with biscuits or toast.

Fish Pie

1 lb (500 g) cod (or whiting, hake, haddock or coley)
1 lb (500 g) smoked haddock
2 bay leaves
½ pint (300 ml) skimmed milk
1 lb (500 g) Jerusalem artichokes, peeled
1½ lb (750 g) potatoes, peeled
1 oz (25 g) butter
1 oz (25 g) plain flour
generous handful of parsley, chopped
sea salt and freshly ground black pepper

Place all the fish in an oven dish with the bay leaves. Pour over the milk and cook in a low oven, 325°F/160°C/gas 3 for 20 minutes. Take out, cool, drain off and reserve the milk and liquor, then discard all the skin and bones. Put the pieces of fish in a pie dish.

Boil the Jerusalem artichokes and the potatoes separately. Drain well. Slice the artichokes thickly and add them to the fish in the pie dish. Mash the potatoes.

Make a roux with the butter and flour, then add the milky liquor the fish was cooked in and the chopped parsley and seasoning. When the sauce is smooth and thick, pour it over the contents in the pie dish. Arrange the mashed potato over the top and bake in a preheated oven, 400°F/200°C/gas 6, for 30 minutes.

Braised Fennel

2 fennel roots, trimmed and quartered
1 oz (25 g) butter
sea salt and freshly ground black pepper

Place the fennel roots on some foil with the butter and the seasoning. Wrap them so that they are completely enclosed in foil and bake in a preheated oven, 400°F/200°C/gas 6, for 30 minutes. (They can go in the oven beneath the fish pie.)

Saturday

BREAKFAST

Marinated cereal

Herb tea

LUNCH

Hummus with cumin

Wholemeal pitta bread

DINNER PARTY

Herb noodles in sesame sauce

•

Asparagus filo pie

Mange-touts

•

Green salad

•

Baked glazed pineapple

Hummus with Cumin

6 oz (175 g) chick peas, soaked overnight
3 cloves of garlic, crushed
juice and zest of 1 lemon
6 fl oz (175 ml) olive oil
2 teaspoons ground cumin
good handful of mint, chopped finely
sea salt and freshly ground black pepper

Cook the chick peas in fresh water for 1½–2 hours or until they are tender. Chick peas do not disintegrate if they are overcooked but they will break up on the point of a knife. Drain them well but reserve about ¼ pint (150 ml) of the cooking liquor, for some of it may be needed if the purée is too thick. Blend the chick peas with all the remaining ingredients until you have a smooth, creamy purée. Chill well before serving.

Herb Noodles in Sesame Sauce

1½ lb (750 g) dried wholewheat or buckwheat noodles
2 tablespoons tahini
1 tablespoon lemon juice
2 tablespoons water
sea salt and freshly ground black pepper
generous bunch of mint, chopped finely
generous bunch of chives, chopped finely

Pour boiling water over the noodles and leave covered for 5 minutes. Mix the tahini with the lemon juice, water and seasoning. Stir thoroughly. Drain the noodles well, add the chopped herbs and tahini sauce and toss so that the noodles are well covered.

Asparagus Filo Pie

1½ lb (750 g) asparagus spears
5 oz (150 g) curd or ricotta cheese
3 tablespoons Greek yoghurt or fromage frais
1 egg, beaten
sea salt and freshly ground black pepper
corn oil
1 lb (500 g) packet of filo pastry
a little milk, for glazing
1 tablespoon sesame seeds

Steam the asparagus spears; then cut into chunks, discarding any fibrous ends. Place in a mixing bowl with the curd or ricotta cheese, Greek yoghurt or fromage frais, beaten egg and seasoning.

Pour a little oil onto a baking tray. Lay out the first 2 filo sheets, oil the top surface and lay out 2 or 3 more, continuing for about 10 sheets. Then spread the asparagus mixture over the filo to within ½ in (1 cm) of the edges. Place 2 sheets of filo over the mixture, oil them, then continue with 2 or 3 more. Go on for 10–12 sheets.

Brush the top with a little milk and scatter with sesame seeds. Bake in a preheated oven, 400°F/200°C/gas 6, for 40 minutes or until golden brown and crunchy. Leave to rest for 5 minutes before slicing and serving.

Serve with the mange-touts which have been steamed for no longer than 3 minutes.

Baked Glazed Pineapple

2 ripe pineapples
2–3 tablespoons honey

Quarter the pineapples, leaving the skin on. Cut each piece across like a melon and place in an oven dish. Pour the honey over each slice and bake at the top of a hot oven, 375°F/190°C/gas 5, for 10 minutes.

Sunday

BRUNCH

Stuffed bread

Lasagne verde

Salade niçoise

Melon, lychee and cherry salad

Kir

SUPPER

Cauliflower cheese

Stuffed Bread

FOR THE BREAD
1 lb (500 g) wholemeal flour
1 teaspoon salt
2 tablespoons olive
1 sachet of micronized yeast
scant ½ pint (300 ml) warm water
egg, beaten, for glazing
poppy seeds

FOR THE STUFFING
2 onions, chopped
5 cloves of garlic, crushed
2–3 stalks of celery, chopped finely
2 oz (50 g) butter, softened
sea salt and freshly ground black pepper

Make the bread by mixing the flour, salt, oil and yeast together thoroughly, then add the water. Knead for 8–10 minutes and then cover and allow the dough to prove for 1 hour. When it has risen, roll the dough out into a rectangle.

Mix the onions, garlic and celery with the softened butter and seasoning and lay the mixture in a column down the centre of the dough. With a sharp knife, cut the sides of the dough into fingers up to the stuffing. Then wrap each finger over the stuffing and tuck in the opposite finger so that there is a lattice pattern.

Place on a greased baking tray, cover and leave to prove for another hour. Brush the top with beaten egg and sprinkle with some poppy seeds. Bake in a preheated oven, 350°F/180°C/gas 4, for 40 minutes.

Lasagne Verde

1½ lb (750 g) broccoli
1 lb (500 g) courgettes
2 lb (1 kg) fresh peas
12–14 strips of lasagne
1–2 tablespoons oil
8 oz (250 g) Parmesan, grated
8 oz (250 g) Gruyère, grated
freshly ground black pepper
1 oz (25 g) butter
2 oz (50 g) plain flour
1¼ pints (750 ml) skimmed milk
8 oz (250 g) matured Cheddar, grated

Cut the florets from the broccoli. Peel the stems and slice them thinly. Poach or steam the stems and florets until al dente. Slice the courgettes crossways, pod the peas, and steam both. Add the courgettes to the broccoli. Blend the peas with ½ pint (300 ml) skimmed milk into a thin purée.

Cook the lasagne sheets in lots of salted, boiling water and 1 tablespoon of oil. Depending on the thickness of the sheets, they will take any time between 5 and 20 minutes to cook. Follow the instructions on the packet.

Have a bowl of cold water with a little oil in it ready. Take the lasagne sheets from the saucepan and put them into the cold water. Drain them on cloths and absorbent paper.

Butter a shallow dish and line the bottom and sides with the lasagne. Add half the grated Parmesan and Gruyère to the broccoli and courgettes, stir it well, then spread over the lasagne. Pour the pea purée over the top and season with the black pepper. You will not need salt because of the Parmesan.

Place another layer of lasagne over the top. Make a thick cheese sauce with the butter, flour, remaining milk, and rest of the grated cheeses. Season with pepper and a little salt. When it has thickened, allow it to cool and then pour it over the top of the pasta. Cook in a preheated oven, 400°F/200°C/gas 6, for 45 minutes–1 hour or until the top is golden brown.

Salad Niçoise

1 large cos lettuce
14 oz (395 g) can of tuna fish (in brine), drained
2 cans of anchovies, drained
2 onions, chopped finely
12 black olives, stoned
2 tablespoons capers
1½ lb (750 g) tomatoes
6 hard-boiled eggs, shelled and halved
juice and zest of 1 lemon
3–4 tablespoons olive oil

FOR THE GARLIC CROÛTONS
3 cloves of garlic, peeled
2 tablespoons olive oil
2–3 slices of wholemeal bread, cubed

Separate the leaves of the lettuce and arrange them fan-shaped in a very large bowl, so that there is plenty of room in the centre.

Flake the tuna and chop the anchovies. Pile them in the centre of the lettuce with the onions, olives and capers. Quarter the tomatoes and place them around the fish. Arrange the hard-boiled egg halves over both.

Make the croûtons by crushing the garlic into the olive oil in a pan. Heat and add the cubed wholemeal bread. Sauté briskly, shaking the pan, until golden brown. Pour the croûtons over the salad.

Mix the lemon juice, zest and oil to make a vinaigrette. Pour over the salad at the table and toss well.

Melon, Lychee and Cherry Salad

2 small, ripe melons
1 lb (500 g) lychees
1 lb (500 g) red cherries

Peel and seed the melon, and cut into chunks. Peel the lychees. Mix both in a large bowl and add the cherries. This fruit salad is so sweet in itself, it needs no added sugar or honey. I do not bother to stone the lychees or cherries.

Cauliflower Cheese

1 large cauliflower
1 oz (25 g) butter
1 oz (25 g) plain flour
½ pint (300 ml) skimmed milk
4 oz (125 g) matured Cheddar, grated
1 tablespoon whole grain mustard like moutarde de Meaux
sea salt and freshly ground black pepper

Cut the florets from the cauliflower and steam them briefly for 5 minutes.
    Make a roux with the butter and flour. Add the milk, cheese, mustard and seasoning. Stir to a smooth sauce. Arrange the cauliflower in an oven dish, pour over the sauce and bake in a preheated oven, 400°F/200°C/gas 6, for 10 minutes.

A WORKING PERSON'S GUIDE TO SPRING

Breakfast and lunch in spring should be very much a personal choice from the ideas and dishes mentioned here, based upon fresh fruit for breakfast and salad for lunch.

Dinner can be helped by having some stores ready in the refrigerator as well as the larder. Smoked tofu is amazingly good and will keep in its vacuum-sealed packet. Haloumi cheese from Cyprus also keeps well and makes a delicious quick snack when grilled. If you have a small freezer, it can contain broad beans, petit pois and spinach – though fresh spinach is far superior. The larder can stock cans of beans in many varieties, canned tomatoes and purée, as well as tuna and anchovies for a quick salad niçoise.

All the grain pilafs are much helped if you add a few tablespoons of cooked beans mixed with some chopped herbs. Canned beans are useful for their quickness – the rest can be kept in the refrigerator and used in another dish later in the week.

Dinner

MONDAY

Stir-fried prawns and vegetables

Rice

Fruit and cheese

TUESDAY

Leek soufflé

Baked potatoes

Avocado and spinach salad

WEDNESDAY

Grilled scallops with couscous pilaf

Broad beans in parsley sauce

THURSDAY

Spiced Bean Croûte

Mixed green salad

FRIDAY

Monkfish kebab

Millet pilaf with beans

MONDAY

Stir-fried Prawns and Vegetables

1 tablespoon corn oil
2–3 slivers each of garlic and fresh root ginger
8 oz (250 g) courgettes, cut thinly in strips
1 carrot, cut thinly in strips
½ bunch of spring onions, chopped finely
1 pint (600 ml) prawns, peeled
2 tablespoons soy sauce
2 tablespoons dry vermouth or sherry

Heat the oil in a wok over high heat, add the garlic and ginger and cook for a moment. Then add the courgettes and carrot and stir-fry for 2–3 minutes. Add the prawns and stir-fry for another minute. Add the spring onions, soy sauce and vermouth or sherry. Stir-fry for 1 minute before serving.

TUESDAY

Leek Soufflé

1 lb (500 g) leeks, trimmed, cleaned and sliced
½ oz (15 g) butter
½ oz (15 g) plain flour
¼ pint (150 ml) skimmed milk
2 oz (50 g) Gruyère, grated
sea salt and freshly ground black pepper
3 eggs, separated

Steam the leeks. Make a roux with the butter and flour, add the milk, cheese and seasoning, and stir until you have a smooth sauce. Let it cool, then stir in the egg yolks and the leeks. Whip the egg whites until stiff and fold them into the mixture.

Butter a soufflé dish. Preheat the oven to 425°F/220°C/gas 7. Pour the mixture into the dish and bake for 20 minutes. Don't open the door while the soufflé is cooking. The soufflé should have risen but the centre should still be runny.

Avocado and Spinach Salad

4 oz (125 g) fresh young spinach leaves
½ ripe avocado, peeled and sliced
1 tablespoon pistachio nuts
1 tablespoon sour cream
1 tablespoon lemon juice
1 tablespoon hazelnut or olive oil
sea salt and freshly ground black pepper

Wash and dry the spinach. Place in a bowl with the avocado slices and scatter over the nuts. Mix the sour cream, lemon juice, oil and seasoning together and pour over the salad.

WEDNESDAY

Grilled Scallops with Couscous Pilaf

3 oz (75 g) couscous
1 small green pepper, cored, seeded and chopped
1 small onion, sliced finely
sea salt and freshly ground black pepper
2–3 scallops
1 tablespoon corn oil

Place the couscous in a colander and pour water over it. Leave to stand for 20 minutes, raking it a few times with your fingers to break up the lumps. Pour into a steamer and add the vegetables and seasoning. Steam for 20 minutes. Meanwhile, detach the coral and slice the scallops in two and paint them with the oil. Grill for 2 minutes on each side. Serve on top of the couscous pilaf.

Broad Beans in Parsley Sauce

1 lb (500 g) broad beans
1 oz (25 g) butter
1 oz (25 g) plain flour
8 fl oz (250 ml) skimmed milk
handful of parsley, finely chopped

Pod the beans and boil them in a little salted water until tender – about 5 minutes. Meanwhile, melt the butter, add the flour and make a roux. Slowly add the milk, stirring until you have a smooth sauce. Add the parsley and seasoning. Drain the beans, place them in a serving dish, and pour the sauce over them.

One of the great fusions of flavours, parsley being a far better herb for broad beans than summer savory which the French use.

THURSDAY

Spiced Bean Croûte

½ small wholemeal loaf
olive oil
14 oz (395 g) can of red kidney beans
1 small can of tomatoes
1 dried red chilli, broken and seeds removed
1 tablespoon tomato purée
2 oz (50 g) smoked tofu, diced
sea salt and freshly ground black pepper

This may only be an up-market version of baked beans on toast but the smoked tofu ups the protein and is far superior to nasty bits of frankfurter sausage.

Cut the crusts off the loaf and cut it into a barrel shape, then cut out from the centre a large circular hole. Paint the croûte with oil and bake in a medium oven, 400°F/200°C/gas 6, to crisp up, about 10–12 minutes.

Drain the beans and tomatoes, mix together and stir in the red chilli. Heat in a pan with the tomato purée and diced tofu, season and then fill the croûte with the mixture.

FRIDAY

Monkfish Kebab

8 oz (250 g) monkfish
1 green pepper, cored and seeded
4 oz (125 g) mushrooms
oil
sea salt and freshly ground black pepper

Cut the fish into chunks. Cut the pepper into square pieces and take the stalks from the mushrooms. Skewer the fish, mushrooms and pepper alternately. Paint the kebabs with oil and season.

Place under a hot grill for 5 minutes, turning the skewer so that all the sides are brown.

Millet Pilaf with Beans

4 oz (125 g) French beans, trimmed
1 onion, sliced
3 oz (75 g) millet
sea salt and freshly ground black pepper
3 tablespoons cooked flageolet beans

Cut the French beans into chunks. Put in a pan with the onion and millet, pour on boiling water to cover and simmer for 10 minutes. When done, drain (if all the water has not been absorbed), season and stir in the flageolet beans.

SUMMER

Introduction

The meals in summer become lighter still. I have left the choice of a light breakfast open – fruit juice is always refreshing, as is a tisane or herb tea, but whether people need something solid is a matter of personal choice.

I have specified salads for lunch, as in spring, for we are certainly more energetic in the summer if we have a light, refreshing daytime meal. Salad fits the bill completely and the choice is infinite.

I love cold soups and avocado makes the best chilled soup of all. Gazpacho is also a favourite, but it is only really good if the tomatoes are ripe and full of flavour.

Salmon is the great fish of summer. For a dinner party, you could poach a whole one and have it cold with a herb mayonnaise. But there are plenty of other recipes for poaching salmon and so I have used salmon steaks as a more economical gesture for the summer dinner party. Cooking food en papillote is a favourite medium, for it encloses the food in a parcel, thus retaining all the juices and flavours. When the parcels are individual, as they are in my recipe, each person can open one at the table to enjoy its flavours immediately.

There are few eggs in these recipes, as the egg yolk is high in cholesterol. I have used some, here and there, for their binding properties as well as for their flavour. But occasionally it is good to have a thoroughly simple egg dish and for the Saturday light lunch they are scrambled with fresh herbs. An omelette au fine herbes would do just as well but it uses rather more butter and takes a little more time if cooking four of them. If you have a garden, do grow lovage amongst your herbs, for a few leaves of this, mixed with the more common herbs like parsley and mint, add a lot more intensity of flavour.

Monday

BREAKFAST

Choice of:

Fresh fruit juice

Herb tea

Wholemeal toast

Fresh fruit

LUNCH

Spinach, lettuce and mushroom salad

Wholemeal bread (page 22)

DINNER

Crab pâté

•

Pancakes stuffed with asparagus and broad beans

New potatoes with mint

•

Cheese and fresh fruit

Spinach, Lettuce and Mushroom Salad

4 oz (125 g) young spinach leaves
1 crisp lettuce
4 oz (125 g) mushrooms, sliced finely
2 oz (50 g) mixed chopped nuts
1 tablespoon freshly grated Parmesan
1 tablespoon lemon juice
3 tablespoons olive oil
1 tablespoon Greek yoghurt
sea salt and freshly ground black pepper

Tear the spinach leaves and lettuce into small scraps. Place in a bowl and scatter the mushrooms and nuts over them. Sprinkle with the Parmesan.

Mix the lemon, oil and yoghurt together. Season and pour over the salad just before serving.

Crab Pâté

1 large crab, boiled
1 oz (25 g) butter
1 oz (25 g) plain flour
¼ pint (150 ml) skimmed milk
1 egg
pinch of sea salt
freshly ground black pepper

To extract the meat from a boiled crab, snap off the legs from the body and reserve them.

Next the gills: sometimes a fishmonger will prise the top of the crab away and remove the gills himself – these are also called dead man's fingers. But they are easily seen, a rather dingy, light brown fringe around the rim of the shell. Cut these away.

The rest of the meat inside, the brown meat, can all be eaten.

The white crab meat is inside the legs and claws. Crack these with a hammer and extract the flesh with a skewer or, better still, a crab or lobster tool specially designed for the purpose.

Once you have the meat out of the crab, mix both brown and white meats together in a bowl to a rough purée.

Make a roux with the butter and flour, add the milk to the pan and make a smooth sauce. Remove from the heat and add it to the crab. Beat in the egg and season.

Pour into a small buttered oven dish, place in a bain-marie and bake in a preheated oven, 400°F/200°C/gas 6, for 20 minutes. Leave to cool before unmoulding.

Pancakes stuffed with Asparagus and Broad Beans

FOR THE PANCAKE BATTER
4 oz (125 g) plain flour
4 oz (125 g) wholemeal flour
½ teaspoon salt
2 eggs
½ pint (300 ml) skimmed milk
½ pint (300 ml) water

FOR THE FILLING
1 lb (500 g) broad beans in their shells
8 oz (250 g) asparagus spears
3 oz (75 g) curd cheese
3 tablespoons quark, Greek yoghurt or fromage frais
2 tablespoons chopped chives
sea salt and freshly ground black pepper

FOR THE TOMATO SAUCE
2 lb (1 kg) tomatoes
3 cloves of garlic, crushed
3 fl oz (75 ml) dry sherry
sea salt and freshly ground black pepper

First make the pancakes. Sift the flours into a mixing bowl and pour back the bran from the sieve. Add the salt. Make a well in the centre and break in the eggs. Mix together so that there is a thick paste. Combine the milk and water and slowly add to the paste, whisking until you have a thin batter. Continue to whisk for a few minutes so that the batter is bubbly. Leave to rest for 1 hour before use and whisk again immediately before using. Make the pancakes in the usual way (this mixture will make 8 pancakes) and stack between greaseproof paper.

Make the filling. Pod the broad beans and cook them in a little salted water. Steam or boil the asparagus, then chop the spears roughly, discarding any fibrous ends. Combine the drained beans and asparagus with all the other filling ingredients.

Place about 1½ heaped tablespoons of the vegetable mixture on each pancake, roll up, then place in an oven dish in a single layer.

Slice the tomatoes in half. Pop them in a pan with the rest of the sauce ingredients. Cook over a low heat, covered, for 10 minutes. Cool, sieve, discard the debris and reheat the liquor. Dribble a little of the tomato sauce over the pancakes and reheat in a hot oven, 425°F/220°C/gas 7, for 10 minutes.

Tuesday

BREAKFAST

Choice of:

Fresh fruit juice

Herb tea

Wholemeal toast

Fresh fruit

LUNCH

Cottage cheese and cucumber salad

Wholemeal bread (page 22)

DINNER

Chilled avocado and lemon soup

•

Kedgeree

Poached fennel

•

Cheese and fresh fruit

Cottage Cheese and Cucumber Salad

5 oz (150 g) cottage cheese
2 oz (50 g) broken walnuts
2 tablespoons chopped parsley
1 cucumber, sliced
sea salt and freshly ground black pepper

Mix the cottage cheese with the walnuts and parsley. Pile in the middle of a plate and surround with the sliced cucumber. Sprinkle with a little seasoning.

Chilled Avocado and Lemon Soup

3 small or 2 large ripe avocados
juice and zest of 2 lemons
3 pints (1.8 litres) soya milk (unsweetened)
sea salt
½ teaspoon ground white pepper
¼ pint (150 ml) sour cream or fromage frais

Peel and stone the avocados and place the flesh in a blender with the juice and zest of 1 lemon, soya milk, sea salt and white pepper. Blend to a purée.

Pour the sour cream into a separate bowl, and add the juice and zest of the second lemon. Mix well together.

Refrigerate the soup for a couple of hours and serve with the sour cream and lemon mixture in a separate bowl for people to help themselves.

Kedgeree

2 lb (1 kg) finnan haddock
4 oz (125 g) butter
3 hard-boiled eggs
6 oz (175 g) Patna rice
generous handful of parsley, chopped
sea salt and freshly ground black pepper
2 eggs, beaten

Place the fish in a saucepan together with 1 oz (25 g) of the butter. Place a lid on the pan and cook over low heat for 15 minutes. Leave to cool, then bone and skin the fish. Peel and chop the hard-boiled eggs finely, and add to the fish.

Pour some boiling water into a pan and cook the rice with a little salt, letting it simmer until just done, about 10 minutes. Put the rice in a metal colander and let it dry out in a low oven for 5 minutes. Melt the remaining butter in a pan and add the fish, chopped egg and rice. Give everything a good stir over a low heat. Add the parsley and a lot of freshly ground black pepper. When the dish is hot, pour in the beaten eggs and stir until they are cooked. Serve at once.

Poached Fennel

3–4 heads fennel
juice and zest of 1 lemon
¼ pint (150 ml) vegetable stock
1 oz (25 g) butter
sea salt and freshly ground black pepper

Trim and quarter the fennel, cutting the feathery tops off and reserving for garnish. In a large pan, put the lemon juice, zest, stock, butter and seasoning. Bring to the boil and lay the fennel, cut side down, in the stock. Simmer for 3 minutes and no longer. Take out the fennel and garnish with the fennel green tops.
Optional: If wished, the stock can be reduced to a few tablespoons and poured over the fennel or it can be reserved for soup.
Note: Kohlrabi can be cooked in the same manner.

Wednesday

BREAKFAST

Choice of:

Fresh fruit juice

Herb tea

Wholemeal toast

Fresh fruit

LUNCH

Fennel, tomato and watercress salad

Wholemeal bread (page 22)

DINNER

Gazpacho

•

Spinach and fresh pea mould

New potatoes with herbs and garlic

•

Cheese and fresh fruit

Fennel, Tomato and Watercress Salad

½ iceberg lettuce
2 fennel roots, chopped
8 oz (250 g) tomatoes, chopped
½ bunch watercress, stalks removed
1 teaspoon lemon juice
1 teaspoon celery salt
1 tablespoon olive oil

Arrange the lettuce leaves in a large bowl. Pile the fennel and tomato in the middle. Encircle with sprigs of watercress. Mix the lemon juice, celery salt and olive oil together and pour over the salad.

Gazpacho

2 lb (1 kg) ripe juicy tomatoes, peeled
1 cucumber
1 onion
1 green pepper, cored and seeded
1 red pepper, cored and seeded
2 cloves of garlic, crushed
2 tablespoons finely chopped parsley
¼ pint (150 ml) olive oil
juice and zest of 2 lemons
2 pints (1.2 litres) vegetable stock
pinch of cayenne
1 teaspoon paprika
sea salt and freshly ground black pepper

FOR SERVING
few ice cubes

Grate the cucumber and onion into a bowl. Either chop the rest of the vegetables up finely or blend them with all the remaining ingredients. Refrigerate for an hour and float the ice cubes on top of the soup before serving.

Spinach and Fresh Pea Mould

1½ lb (750 g) spinach leaves
3 oz (75 g) goat's cheese
sea salt and freshly ground black pepper
2 eggs
2 lb (1 kg) peas in their pods
3 oz (75 g) feta cheese

Wash the spinach and cook it without water over low heat. When it is tender, chop it roughly and put into a mixing bowl. Add the goat's cheese, seasoning and 1 egg. Mix thoroughly. Pod the peas, boil until tender, drain and blend in a liquidizer with the feta, 1 egg and some pepper.

Butter a 2½ pint (1.5 litre) soufflé dish or mould. Place half the spinach at the bottom, pour over the pea mixture, then top with the rest of the spinach.

Place the mould in a bain-marie, protect the top with buttered paper and bake in a preheated oven, 425°F/220°C/gas 7, for 30–40 minutes. Leave to rest for 5 minutes before unmoulding.

New Potatoes with Herbs and Garlic

1 oz (25 g) butter
2 tablespoons olive oil
5 cloves garlic, minced or finely chopped
generous handful of parsley, basil and mint mixed and finely chopped
3 tablespoons fine wholemeal breadcrumbs
sea salt and freshly ground black pepper
2 lb (1 kg) new potatoes, scrubbed and steamed

Melt the butter and heat the olive oil in a pan. Throw in the garlic and sweat it for a few minutes. Add the herbs, breadcrumbs and seasoning. Stir well, then throw in the new potatoes. Turn the potatoes so that they are covered in the mixture and place under a hot grill so that the breadcrumbs are toasted. Serve as soon as possible.

Thursday

BREAKFAST

Choice of:

Fresh fruit juice

Herb tea

Wholemeal toast

Fresh fruit

LUNCH

Broad bean, tomato and onion salad

Wholemeal bread (page 22)

DINNER

Peppers stuffed with smoked aubergine

•

Macaroni and broccoli cheese

•

Fruit tofu salad

Broad Bean, Tomato and Onion Salad

1½ lb (750 g) broad beans
8 oz (250 g) tomatoes, sliced
1 bunch of spring onions, chopped
1 tablespoon lemon juice
3 tablespoons olive oil
sea salt and freshly ground black pepper
1 small iceberg lettuce

Pod the beans and cook them in boiling water until tender. Drain and place in a bowl with the tomatoes and spring onions. Mix the lemon juice, oil and seasoning together and pour over the salad.

Arrange the lettuce leaves in a bowl and pile the salad in the middle.

Peppers stuffed with Smoked Aubergine

2–3 small aubergines
3 tablespoons olive oil
4 cloves of garlic, crushed
1 onion, chopped
1 green chilli, chopped
2 oz (50 g) fresh root ginger, grated
1 teaspoon each of mustard seeds, cumin seeds and asafoetida
juice and zest of 1 lemon
sea salt and freshly ground black pepper
4–6 medium green peppers
¼ pint (150 ml) dry white wine
¼ pint (150 ml) vegetable stock

First smoke the aubergines. Prick them with a fork and grill them, charring the skin. Turn them over on all sides so that the outside blisters and blackens and the inside becomes soft.

Leave to cool and scrape away the blackened skin. Extract all the pulp and chop it roughly.

Heat the olive oil in a pan and add the garlic, onion, chilli, ginger, mustard seeds, cumin and asafoetida. Cook for a few moments until the onion softens, then add the aubergine pulp. Stir thoroughly and cook for a further few minutes before adding the lemon juice and seasoning.

Prepare the peppers by slicing the tops off and scooping out the core and seeds.

Choose an oven dish with a lid which will neatly hold all the peppers and keep them upright. Pour in the white wine and stock. Fill each pepper with the filling. Place its lid on and fit into the oven dish. Bake in a preheated oven, 275°F/190°C/gas 5, for 30–40 minutes.

Serve at once.

Macaroni and Broccoli Cheese

4 oz (125 g) wholewheat macaroni
1½ lb (750 g) broccoli or calabrese
1 oz (25 g) butter
1 oz (25 g) plain flour
½ pint (300 ml) skimmed milk
4 oz (125 g) matured Gouda (or other hard, low fat cheese), grated
sea salt and freshly ground black pepper

Boil the macaroni until tender. Drain and reserve. Peel the stalks of the broccoli or calabrese. Cut the florets away and boil or steam both until tender. Drain and reserve.

Make a roux with the butter and flour, then add the milk, cheese and seasoning. Stir until you have a smooth sauce.

Butter an oven dish, pour the macaroni in, arrange the vegetables over it, then pour over the sauce. Bake in a preheated oven, 400°F/200°C/gas 6, for 10 minutes.

Fruit Tofu Salad

1 dessert apple
1 dessert pear
2–3 plums
2–3 nectarines or peaches (unskinned and chopped roughly)
1 packet tofu (morinaga)
2 tablespoons honey
1 tablespoon soft brown sugar

Place the chopped fruit in a bowl. Drain the tofu and blend it with the honey. Beat the chopped fruit into it and sprinkle the top with the sugar. Chill before serving.

Friday

BREAKFAST

Choice of:

Fresh fruit juice

Herb tea

Wholemeal toast

Fresh fruit

LUNCH

Fresh pea, feta and tomato salad

Wholemeal bread (page 22)

DINNER

Kipper pâté

•

Cannelloni stuffed with mushrooms and laver

•

Cheese and fresh fruit

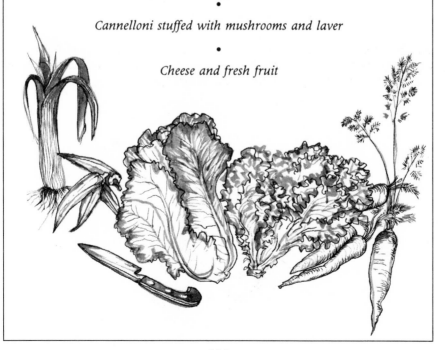

Fresh Pea, Feta and Tomato Salad

1 lb (500 g) peas in their pods
4 oz (125 g) feta cheese
1 cos lettuce
1 onion, sliced finely
1 lb (500 g) tomatoes, chopped
6 black olives, stoned
1 tablespoon lemon juice
3 tablespoons olive oil
sea salt and freshly ground black pepper

Shell the peas and cook until tender. Break up the feta. Separate the leaves of the cos lettuce and arrange them in a bowl. Mix everything else together and pile it into the centre.

Kipper Pâté

2 pairs of undyed oak-smoked kippers
2 oz (50 g) butter, softened
1 tablespoon Worcestershire sauce
1 tablespoon lemon juice
Lots of freshly ground black pepper

Steam the kippers for 10 minutes. Leave to cool, then take the flesh from the bones and skin. Place the flesh in a blender and purée with the rest of the ingredients. Refrigerate for a few hours before using.

Cannelloni stuffed with Mushrooms and Laver

8–10 sheets of cannelloni
1 oz (25 g) butter
8 oz (250 g) mushrooms, sliced finely
2 cans of laver bread
1 bunch of spring onions, chopped finely
5 oz (150 g) curd cheese

FOR THE PARSLEY SAUCE
1 oz (25 g) butter
1 oz (25 g) plain flour
¾ pint (450 ml) skimmed milk
sea salt and freshly ground black pepper
generous handful of parsley, chopped finely

Boil the cannelloni until tender and drain well. Melt the butter in a pan. Throw in the mushrooms and cook over low heat until tender. Pour into a mixing bowl and add the laver, spring onions and cheese. Mix thoroughly. Fill the cannelloni with the mixture, rolling them up neatly. Place in a buttered oven dish, closely packed.

Make a roux with the butter and flour, then add the milk, seasoning and parsley. Stir until the sauce is smooth. Dribble the sauce over the cannelloni and bake in a preheated oven, 400°F/200°C/gas 6, for 20–25 minutes.

Saturday

BREAKFAST

Choice of:

Fresh fruit juice

Herb tea

Wholemeal toast (page 22)

Fresh fruit

LUNCH

Scrambled eggs with herbs

Wholemeal toast

DINNER PARTY

Summer vegetable terrine

Orange and onion sauce

•

Salmon steaks wrapped in lettuce

Quick hollandaise sauce

New potatoes with mint

Peas

Cucumber salad

•

Summer pudding

Scrambled Eggs with Herbs

1 oz (25 g) butter
6 eggs, beaten
3 tablespoons finely chopped parsley
3 tablespoons finely chopped mint
3 tablespoons finely chopped chives
sea salt and freshly ground black pepper

Melt the butter in a frying pan and pour in the eggs, then tip in the herbs
and seasoning. Beat with a fork and take away from the heat while the
centre of the eggs are still slightly liquid. They will set in their own warmth
and this stops the dish being too dry.

Have the toast ready, hot and buttered.

Summer Vegetable Terrine

1 lb (500 g) broad beans (weight after podding)
1 lb (500 g) carrots
4 oz (125 g) curd cheese
2 eggs
sea salt and freshly ground black pepper
1 oz (25 g) pistachio nuts, shelled and skinned

Cook the broad beans in a little salted water until tender; drain, and
liquidize them to a purée with half of the curd cheese and 1 of the eggs.
Season and put to one side. Then boil the carrots until tender and liquidize
with the rest of the curd cheese, the other egg and seasoning.

Butter a terrine and line it with buttered greaseproof paper or put in a
foil handle to help unmould the terrine. (Take a long strip of foil, butter the
middle part and put it lengthways in the dish. Put in the terrine, then twist
the ends to strengthen them, and once the buttered paper is in place, fold
them over during cooking. If you don't twist the ends they are liable to
tear.) Place a layer of the broad bean purée in the base, then all of the carrot
purée. Scatter the pistachio nuts over and press them down. Finish by
covering with the rest of the broad bean purée.

Protect with buttered paper and place in a bain-marie. Cook in a
preheated oven, 400°F/200°C/gas 6, for 30 minutes. Leave to rest before
unmoulding. Serve with the orange and onion sauce.

Orange and Onion Sauce

1 oz (25 g) butter
2 large onions, sliced finely
Juice and zest of 1 orange
sea salt and freshly ground black pepper

Melt the butter in a pan, and add the onions, orange juice and zest. Cook over a low heat for 10 minutes or until the onions are transparent. Pour into a liquidizer and blend to a smooth purée. Reheat the sauce gently and check for seasoning.

Salmon Steaks wrapped in Lettuce

6–8 large lettuce leaves
6–8 salmon steaks
1 tablespoon butter
3 tablespoons chopped dill
sea salt and freshly ground black pepper

Blanch the lettuce leaves for a moment, then drain them. Place a salmon steak on each lettuce leaf, smear it with a little butter, sprinkle with a little dill and seasoning, then wrap the lettuce closely around.

Butter an oval dish. Place the parcels in the dish, cover with buttered paper or foil and cook in a preheated oven, 400°F/200°C/gas 6, for 20 minutes. This is good hot or cold. Serve with quick hollandaise sauce.

Quick Hollandaise Sauce

Place 2 egg yolks in the blender. Add 2 tablespoons of lemon juice and the zest of 1 lemon.

Melt 4 oz (125 g) of butter and add it, bit by bit, to the lemon and yolks with the blender on low speed. Increase the flow of butter as you increase the speed of the machine, until you get a creamy sauce.

Pour into a bowl and serve at once.

Cucumber salad

1 whole cucumber
sea salt
generous handful of mint, chopped finely
1 tablespoon Greek yoghurt
1 teaspoon lemon juice
1 tablespoon olive oil

Score the peel of the cucumber with a fork and slice thinly. Place in a colander and sprinkle with salt, then leave for 1 hour.

Rinse the salt off, drain and pat dry. Mix the rest of the ingredients together, place the cucumber in a bowl and toss in the sauce.

Summer Pudding

1 small white loaf
1 lb (500 g) red currants
1 lb (500 g) raspberries

Cut the loaf into slices. Slice the crusts away and line a large pudding basin with some of the bread. Take trouble to cut and shape the bread at the bottom and sides so that there are no gaps.

Bring the red currants to the boil in a pan (add no water and no sugar), and immediately take away from the heat. Stir in the raspberries and let them get cold. Drain off any excess juice and reserve. Pile the fruit into the lined pudding basin, fill to the top, and cover with more bread. Place a plate and then a weight on top of the basin and refrigerate for 1 day.

Unmould before serving. If there is any bread left unstained with juice, pour some of the reserved juice over, or keep to serve at the table.

Sunday

BRUNCH

Pasta and chick pea salad

Cold vegetable curry

Mixed grain pilaf

Crudités: taramasalata, melitzana and tapenade

Pimms

SUPPER

Pizza

Pasta and Chick Pea Salad

4 oz (125 g) chick peas, soaked overnight
8 oz (250 g) mixed decorative pasta shapes
1 tablespoon lemon juice
3 tablespoons olive oil
1 tablespoon whole grain mustard, such as moutarde de Meaux
1 tablespoon tomato purée
sea salt and freshly ground black pepper
generous bunch of parsley, chopped finely
1 bunch of spring onions, chopped finely

Boil the chick peas in fresh water until tender – it can take up to 2 hours. They do not disintegrate, but break open at the point of a knife. Drain well. Cook the pasta in a pan of boiling water until al dente, about 10 minutes. Drain well and combine with the chick peas.

Make a vinaigrette with the lemon juice, oil, mustard and tomato purée. Pour on to the pasta and chick peas while still warm. Toss well, season, and leave to cool. Add the parsley and spring onions just before serving.

Cold Vegetable Curry

6 oz (175 g) haricot beans, soaked overnight and drained
2 tablespoons corn oil
3 cloves of garlic, crushed
½ teaspoon each of mustard seeds, fenugreek, ground coriander, cardomom seeds and cumin seeds
1 teaspoon each of turmeric and asafoetida
2 onions, chopped finely
2 green peppers, cored, seeded and chopped
2 red peppers, cored, seeded and chopped
2 lb (1 kg) new potatoes, scrubbed and diced
1 lb (500 g) mushrooms, sliced
2 lb (1 kg) courgettes, chopped
sea salt and freshly ground black pepper
2 oz (50 g) creamed coconut, grated

First cook the haricot beans in plenty of water until tender – this will take anything from 45 minutes to 1 hour. Drain and reserve the water.

In a very large casserole or pan, heat the oil. Throw in the garlic and spices. Cook for a moment or two until the mustard seeds pop. Then add all the vegetables (except for the beans), pour the bean water over everything and bring to the boil. Simmer for 20 minutes.

Add the beans and seasoning and cook for another 5 minutes. Then stir in the coconut and cook for another minute. Leave to cool.

Mixed Grain Pilaf

3 oz (75 g) couscous
3 oz (75 g) buckwheat
3 oz (75 g) millet
8 oz (250 g) fresh garden peas
2 green peppers, cored, seeded and diced small
2 onions, sliced thinly
juice of 2 lemons
handful of mint, chopped finely
sea salt and freshly ground black pepper

Pour the water over the couscous, then immediately drain and leave to stand for 15 minutes; crumble the grains in your fingers to break up the lumps before steaming. Boil the buckwheat in a little salted water for 10 minutes. When tender drain and put to one side. Simmer the millet for 20 minutes and steam the couscous over it.

Pod the peas and boil them in a little salted water for 5–8 minutes. Drain and reserve. Drain the millet and combine all the grains in a large bowl. Add the peppers and the peas to the grains together with the onions. Pour the lemon juice over the grains and add the finely chopped mint. Season to taste.

Crudités

Choose vegetables at their peak. Trim and cut them into pieces suitable for finger food. Vegetables like celery, courgettes, carrots and cucumber can often be used as scoops for purées. Plan a mixture of these, plus tiny cherry tomatoes, green, yellow and red peppers, celeriac and avocado (but dip the pieces in lemon juice to stop oxidation), hearts of Little Gem lettuce, trimmed stalks of white and red cabbage, florets of cauliflower, broccoli or calabrese. Arrange them in contrasting colours in a design on a large platter. Marvellous with aioli or mayonnaise as well as the purées suggested here.

Taramasalata

1 lb (500 g) smoked cod's roe
3 cloves of garlic, crushed
2 tablespoons lemon juice
½ pint (300 ml) olive oil
2 oz (50 g) curd cheese
freshly ground black pepper

Scrape the roe from its skin. Discard the skin (or eat it, or give it to the cat). Place the roe in a blender and blend in the garlic, lemon juice and oil bit by bit (as if making mayonnaise). Finally blend in the curd cheese and black pepper.

Melitzana

Oil the skin of 1–2 aubergines and bake in a medium oven, 325°F/170°C/gas 3, for 2–3 hours or until soft. Scrape the flesh from the skin and place in a blender with 3 crushed cloves of garlic, the juice and zest of 1 lemon, ¼ pint (150 ml) olive oil, a little sea salt and freshly ground pepper. Blend until you get a thick purée and then check the seasoning.

Tapenade

10 black olives, stoned
1 can of anchovies
2 tablespoons capers
juice and zest of 1 lemon
5 cloves of garlic, crushed
¼ pint (150 ml) olive oil
sea salt and freshly ground black pepper

Blend everything to a thick purée in a blender, then add black pepper carefully, to taste.

Pizza

FOR THE DOUGH
8 oz (250 g) strong white flour
½ teaspoon salt
1 sachet micronized yeast
2 tablespoons milk, warmed
1 egg, beaten
2 tablespoons olive oil
2–3 tablespoons warm water

FOR THE FILLING
2 tablespoons olive oil
2 onions, sliced
1 green pepper, cored, seeded and sliced
5 cloves of garlic, crushed
1 teaspoon oregano
14 oz (395 g) can of tomatoes
2 tablespoons tomato purée
sea salt and freshly ground black pepper
5 fresh tomatoes, sliced
12 black olives, stoned
4 oz (125 g) mozzarella, sliced

Make the dough. Sieve the flour and the salt into a large mixing bowl. Place the yeast in a cup and pour over the warmed milk. Stir and leave to ferment, about 10 minutes. Once fermented, add the creamed yeast to the flour, then add the beaten egg, olive oil and warm water. Stir well. Knead the dough until it becomes smooth and elastic. Form into a ball and leave in a covered bowl in a warm place for 2 hours, to allow it to rise.

While the dough is rising, make the filling. Heat the olive oil in a pan and add the onions, pepper, garlic and oregano. Cook gently for about 10 minutes, then add the canned tomatoes. Simmer for 45 minutes, by which time you should have a thick sauce. Add the tomato purée and seasoning and cook for another 5 minutes.

Oil a 12 × 14 in (30 × 35 cm) baking sheet. Take the ball of risen dough and smooth it down over the baking sheet, pressing and pulling the dough out. Make a small ridge of dough around the edge of the sheet. Leave to rest for 10 minutes. Spread the filling over the dough, then garnish with slices of fresh tomato, the black olives and sliced mozzarella. Rest the pizza again for 10 minutes.

Bake in a preheated oven, 425°F/220°C/gas 7, for 15 minutes, then turn the oven down to 350°F/180°C/gas 4 and continue baking for another 15 minutes.

A WORKING PERSON'S GUIDE TO SUMMER

However busy and tired you are, it is actually stimulating and refreshes the spirit no end to take time and trouble in presenting a meal for yourself. Summer is full of fresh goodies and so salads should be somewhere at the top of the list in the diet. There are also in the markets now so many new vegetables and salad leaves to buy that salads can look as appealing as a florist's window. The greater the appeal of the dish in the way it looks, the better your digestion will be.

Fresh fish makes a simple meal which is a splendid treat. A Dover sole, plainly grilled with a tiny amount of butter, accompanied by new potatoes and fresh peas, with a quarter of a lemon squeezed over the fish is a meal for a prince. A Dover sole needs nothing but the simplest treatment – doing anything more detracts from the clear, sweet flavour. Dressed crab is another excellent buy; eaten with salad, it makes a superb supper. These fish and others are ideal for the single busy person

Both the pancake batter and the marinated salmon can be prepared the night before.

The number of eggs used in this book is fairly low compared with what was used, say, 10 years ago. For the working person, eggs are immensely useful, as they are quick and nutritious. But do beware that you are not consuming too many. However, there are two egg recipes in this week, partly because piperade is a firm favourite with most people and also because avocado, heated and not cooked, in an omelette is a delicacy not often served.

Dinner

MONDAY

Mixed summer salad

Fruit and cheese

TUESDAY

Piperade

Fruit and cheese

WEDNESDAY

Pancakes stuffed with broad beans

Mixed Salad

Fruit and cheese

THURSDAY

Marinated salmon

Rice salad

Fruit and cheese

FRIDAY

Avocado omelette

Fruit and vegetable salad

Chick peas with garlic croûtons

Cheese

Mixed Summer Salad

1 lb (500 g) asparagus
8 oz (250 g) fresh garden peas
8 oz (250 g) fresh broad beans
few lettuce leaves
½ bunch of spring onions, trimmed
½ oz (15 g) broken walnuts
8 oz (250 g) tomatoes, sliced
few basil leaves, chopped roughly
2 tablespoons walnut oil
1 tablespoon lemon juice
3 tablespoons fromage frais or Greek yoghurt
sea salt and freshly ground black pepper

Trim and steam or boil the asparagus until just tender; drain and cool. Pod and cook the peas and beans until tender; drain and cool.

Lay the lettuce leaves out over a platter. Arrange the asparagus stalks pointing outwards at each end. Arrange the spring onions in 2 bunches on the other sides. Pile the peas and broad beans into the centre, then scatter over the nuts. Ring the centre with the tomatoes and cover them with the basil leaves.

Mix the oil, lemon juice, fromage frais and seasoning together and pour over the centre. Eat this salad with fresh wholemeal bread.

Piperade

2 tablespoons olive oil
2 green peppers, cored, seeded and sliced
1 onion, sliced
2 cloves of garlic, crushed
1 lb (500 g) tomatoes, peeled and chopped
2 eggs
sea salt and freshly ground black pepper

Heat the oil in a shallow pan. Throw in the peppers and the onion. Cook over low heat for about 20 minutes so that the vegetables soften and almost mingle into a purée. Throw in the tomatoes and cook for another 5 minutes, stirring once or twice to make a purée. Now break in the eggs and scramble them into the mixture. Season.

Eat with toast or garlic bread.

Garlic Bread

Use a small French loaf which can be the traditional white or a wholemeal. Slice the loaf across but not entirely through, so that the base is still whole. Crush about 8 or 10 cloves of garlic into 6 oz (150 g) softened butter. Add lots of freshly milled black pepper and a little sea salt and mix thoroughly. Spread the half-severed slices with a generous amount of the garlic butter and close up the loaf. Place it in foil, wrap tightly and put on a baking sheet in a hot oven, 400°F/200°C/gas 6 for 15 minutes. Unwrap and finish cutting the loaf into separate pieces at the table.

WEDNESDAY

Pancakes stuffed with Broad Beans

This is merely a simpler version of the recipe on page 100. Make a quarter of the quantity of the pancake batter the night before.

Pod 8 oz (250 g) of fresh broad beans and cook them. Mix the beans with a few chopped spring onions, some seasoning and 2 tablespoons of fromage frais.

Make 2 pancakes. Heat the broad bean mixture gently, then place on the pancakes and fold them over. Sprinkle with a little grated Parmesan.

THURSDAY

Marinated Salmon

8 oz (250 g) fresh salmon, in 2 cutlets
1 tablespoon sea salt
1 tablespoon caster sugar
¼ pint (150 ml) white wine vinegar
juice and zest of 2 oranges

Skin and bone the salmon and slice each cutlet in two, fairly thinly. Lay them in a shallow dish.

Stir the salt and sugar into the wine vinegar and orange juice until it is dissolved. Pour over the salmon with the orange zest so that the salmon is covered. Refrigerate for 24 hours. The ascorbic acid 'cooks' the salmon and flavours it with orange.

Throw away the marinade and eat the fish with a mixed green salad and a mixed rice salad.

Rice salad

3 oz (75 g) Patna rice
1 red pepper, finely chopped
½ bunch spring onions, finely chopped
¼ cucumber, finely chopped
3 tablespoons hazelnut oil
1 tablespoon lemon juice
sea salt and freshly ground black pepper

Cook the rice until tender. Rinse under a cold tap and drain well. Put it into a bowl and add the vegetables. Make a dressing with the oil and lemon juice and season well. Toss the salad and leave for an hour to allow the rice to soak up the flavours.

Avocado Omelette

3 eggs
sea salt and freshly ground black pepper
1 ripe avocado
1 oz (25 g) butter

Beat the eggs together in a bowl with the seasoning. Peel, stone and slice the avocado. Melt the butter in a pan and pour the egg in; let the bottom set. Lay the avocado slices over half the egg and, after a moment so that the egg just sets around the avocado slices, fold the omelette over and slip it out of the pan onto a plate.

Fruit and Vegetable Salad

Any combination of 3 or 4 fruit and vegetables in a light dressing is delicious: stoned cherries, tomatoes, onion and lettuce, or even a combination of red currants, nasturtiums and cucumber.

Chick Peas with Garlic Croûtons

½ a 14 oz (395 g) can chick peas
2 slices wholemeal bread
3 tablespoons sesame oil
4 cloves of garlic, crushed
2 dried red chillies (optional)
seasoning

Drain the chick peas and place in a bowl. Cut the bread into 1 in (2.5 cm) chunks. Heat the oil in a pan and throw in the garlic and chillies (if you are using them). Sauté briskly until the bread is crisp and brown. Pour contents of the pan over the chick peas and toss thoroughly, adding seasoning to taste.

AUTUMN

Introduction

As we continue into autumn, we start to want warming soups and a little more breakfast. Although, if we have an Indian summer, how good it is to be eating salads out of doors again. Tomatoes are excellent in this season and home-made tomato soup can be one of the most enjoyable dishes of the year, especially if you have grown your own tomatoes. Sweetcorn, globe artichokes and pumpkin are other seasonal vegetables which are a treat. Sweetcorn makes beautiful fritters and moulds, and can also be used as a filling in pancakes. I find it always worthwhile to cook the whole cobs and cut the kernels off. Canned or frozen corn kernels often have added sugar and other preservatives, and generally taste vile.

Though globe artichokes can be eaten with a garlic vinaigrette or a lemon butter sauce, when they are really large I think they are particularly good with their middles plucked out, including the chokes, and stuffed.

Pumpkin soup is a favourite autumn soup. The colour of amber, it tastes like no other soup or vegetable and always slips down a treat. Use pumpkin like marrow or squash – cube it, then fry in corn oil with ginger.

Quinces are my other choice for autumn. Quinces and game go particularly well together; the sharp, lemony flavour of quince is the perfect complement to a wild bird. Sum up the essence of autumn with, at the end of the meal, a glazed apple tart.

Monday

BREAKFAST

Fresh fruit juice

Miso spread with wholemeal toast

Herb tea

LUNCH

Beetroot and chilli soup

Wholemeal bread (page 22)

DINNER

Smoked haddock moulds

•

Mushroom tart

Austrian red cabbage

•

Endive and black-eyed bean salad

•

Cheese and fresh fruit

Miso Spread

To 1 part of miso, add 2 parts of tahini. Mix thoroughly and keep in a covered jar in the refrigerator.

Beetroot and Chilli Soup

This makes a thin, but nourishing, beetroot soup spiced with a little heat.

Peel and chop 2 lb (1 kg) of raw beetroot. Thinly slice 1 large cabbage and 1 lb (500 g) of carrots. Place in a casserole with 2 broken dried red chillies (seeds removed). Cover with water. Bring to the boil with a little sea salt and black pepper. Cook in a preheated oven, 350°F/180°C/gas 4, for 3 hours. Take from the oven and put everything through a sieve. Discard the vegetables.

Serve with a spoonful of yoghurt or sour cream.

Smoked Haddock Moulds

1 oz (25 g) butter
1 large finnan haddock
3 oz (75 g) curd cheese
2 eggs, beaten
generous bunch of parsley, chopped
sea salt and freshly ground black pepper

Melt the butter in a pan. Place the haddock in it and cook over very gentle heat for 8–10 minutes. Cool and then carefully skin and bone the fish. Flake the fish into a bowl and pour the juices over it. Mash the curd cheese into the fish, and add the eggs, parsley and seasoning.

Butter 4–6 ramekins and pour the mixture in. Place the ramekins in a bain-marie, cover with buttered paper, and bake in a preheated, 400°F/200°C/gas 6, for 20 minutes. Unmould when just cool.

Mushroom Tart

1 oz (25 g) butter
8 oz (250 g) mushrooms, sliced thinly
2 egg yolks
½ pint (300 ml) single cream
2 oz (50 g) Gruyère
sea salt and freshly ground black pepper
1 wholemeal pastry case, baked blind (*page 28*)

Heat the butter in a pan and throw in the mushrooms. Sauté until tender –
a few minutes. Mix the egg yolks with the cream and cheese, and add the
mushrooms. Season and pour into the pastry case. Bake in a preheated
oven, 400°F/200°C/gas 6, for 30 minutes.

Austrian Red Cabbage

1 red cabbage, sliced thinly
5 cloves of garlic, sliced thinly
1 teaspoon paprika
2 tablespoons brown sugar
sea salt and freshly ground black pepper
3 fl oz (75 ml) red wine vinegar
3 cooking apples

Place the cabbage and garlic in a casserole. Sprinkle with the paprika, sugar,
salt and pepper. Pour over the red wine vinegar. Core and peel the apples,
slice them and place over the cabbage. Put a lid on the casserole and cover
in a preheated oven, 325°F/170°C/gas 3, for 3 hours.

Endive and Black-eyed Bean Salad

3 oz (75 g) black-eyed beans, soaked overnight
1 tablespoon olive oil
1 teaspoon garam masala
1 teaspoon lemon juice
1 teaspoon honey
sea salt and freshly ground black pepper
endive leaves

Boil the drained beans in fresh water for 30–45 minutes. When tender, drain. Mix the oil, garam masala, lemon juice, honey and seasoning together. While the beans are still hot, toss them thoroughly in this mixture and put aside until they are to be served. Arrange the endive leaves over a large platter and heap the beans, in their vinaigrette, in the centre.

Tuesday

BREAKFAST

Fresh fruit juice

Muesli and yoghurt

Herb tea

LUNCH

Simple French onion soup

Wholemeal bread (page 22)

DINNER

Tomatoes Provençale

•

Swiss chard timbale

Baked spiced potatoes

•

Mixed leaf salad

•

Cheese and fresh fruit

Simple French Onion Soup

1 oz (25 g) butter
3 cloves of garlic, crushed
1½ lb (750 g) onions, sliced finely
1 tablespoon honey
2 pints (1.2 litres) vegetable stock
sea salt and freshly ground black pepper
2 oz (50 g) Gruyère, grated

Heat the butter in a pan, add the garlic and onions and cook over a low heat for 5 minutes. Add the honey and continue to cook for a further 5 minutes. Add the vegetable stock and seasoning. Bring to the boil and simmer for 30 minutes. Stir in the cheese before serving.

Tomatoes Provençale

4–6 large tomatoes
4 cloves of garlic, crushed
2 tablespoons olive oil
2 tablespoons wholemeal breadcrumbs
sea salt and freshly ground black pepper

Slice the tomatoes in half. Score the surface of each in a lattice design, ¼ in (5 mm) deep. Mix the garlic with some salt and pepper and smooth it over the scored surface of the tomatoes. Sprinkle with breadcrumbs and oil and place under a hot grill until the tops are crisp.

Swiss Chard Timbale

1 lb (500 g) Swiss chard
2 oz (50 g) onion, chopped finely
4 eggs, beaten
2 oz (50 g) Cheddar, grated
pinch of nutmeg
sea salt and freshly ground black pepper
½ pint (300 ml) skimmed milk
2 oz (50 g) wholemeal breadcrumbs

Chop the stalks from the Swiss chard leaves. Boil the stalks for 5 minutes in a little salted water, then add the leaves. Continue to cook for another 5 minutes. Leave to cool, drain and place in a blender. Reduce to a rough purée. Transfer to a bowl and stir in the chopped onion, beaten eggs, cheese, nutmeg and seasoning. Then beat in the milk.

Butter a 2½ pint (1.5 litre) mould or soufflé dish and shake in the breadcrumbs. Move the mould around so that the crumbs cover the bottom and sides. Gently pour in the mixture. Cover with buttered paper and place the dish in a bain-marie. Bake in a preheated oven, 375°F/190°C/gas 5, for 30–40 minutes or until the centre is set (place a knife in the centre and if it comes out clean, it is done).

Leave to rest for 5 minutes before unmoulding.

Baked Spiced Potatoes

4–6 large potatoes
2 tablespoons corn oil
½ teaspoon each of mustard seeds and fenugreek
½ pint (300 ml) yoghurt
1 tablespoon curry powder
sea salt

Peel the potatoes and boil them for 5 minutes. Drain them. Heat the oil in a small pan and throw in the mustard and fenugreek seeds. Cook for a moment until the seeds pop.

Mix the seeds with the yoghurt and add the curry powder and salt. Pour into a baking dish, roll the potatoes in the mixture and leave for 30 minutes to absorb it. Bake the potatoes in a preheated oven, 350°F/180°C/gas 4, for 1 hour.

Wednesday

BREAKFAST

Fresh fruit juice

Marinated cereal

Herb tea

LUNCH

Tomato soup

Wholemeal bread (page 22)

DINNER

Sweetcorn moulds

•

Stir-fried duck breasts

Brown rice pilaf

•

Honeyed tofu

Marinated Cereal

2 tablespoons rolled oats
2 tablespoons bulgur wheat
1 tablespoon fresh walnuts, broken
1 teaspoon sunflower seeds
¼ pint (150 ml) fresh apple juice (*see below*)
1 dessert apple, chopped

Prepare this breakfast the night before. Mix the oats, bulgur wheat, walnuts and seeds together. Pour on the juice and leave in the refrigerator overnight. Add the apple in the morning before serving.

Fresh Apple Juice
There are various types of fruit juice extractor machines on the market. Some give you raw juice and another, mentioned below, cooks the juice. Both are of high quality and which one you use depends on what you need the juice for. Obviously, for a quick breakfast cereal, the raw fruit juice is good to have. This type of machine pulps the whole fruit – peel, core and pips – and will give you a thick, tasty juice with the maximum amount of vitamins and minerals. The machine which steams the fruit is the Mehu-Maija and this is particularly useful if you have a glut of apples for it will take large amounts of fruit and, in the process of steaming, syphon off all the juice. This juice can be bottled and stored in the refrigerator for some time.

Tomato Soup

3 lb (1.5 kg) tomatoes
2 cloves of garlic, crushed
handful of fresh basil leaves
sea salt and freshly ground black pepper

Puncture the skin of the tomatoes or cut them in half. Throw them into a pan with the rest of the ingredients and simmer over a very low heat for 10 minutes so that the tomatoes cook in their own juices. Leave to cool, then put through a sieve. Discard the skin and seeds and reheat the tomato liquor gently.

There should be, from this amount of tomatoes, 1½ pints (850 ml) of soup. It is so good that it should never be watered down with a stock.

Sweetcorn Moulds

2 corn cobs
2 large leeks (white part only)
2 eggs, beaten
2 oz (50 g) curd cheese
1 oz (25 g) butter
sea salt and freshly ground black pepper

Cook the corn cobs until tender, about 8 minutes. Butter 4 small ramekin dishes. Take the first 2 outside leaves from each of the leeks and blanch them whole. Drain. Then bisect the leaves with a sharp knife so that you have 4 thin, almost transparent, layers. Arrange them at the bottom and sides of 4 ramekins with enough overlap for the top. Slice the remaining leeks thinly and cook in the butter for a few minutes until tender.

Cut the corn kernels off the cobs. Place in a bowl and add the leeks and the rest of the ingredients. Mix well. Pour into the ramekins and fold over the leek leaves.

Protect the ramekins with buttered paper and place in a bain-marie. Bake in a preheated oven, 375°F/190°C/gas 5, for 20–25 minutes. Allow to rest for 5 minutes before unmoulding.

Stir-fried Duck Breasts

2 duck breasts
seasoned flour
2 tablespoons unrefined sesame oil
4 cloves of garlic, sliced thinly
1 oz (25 g) root ginger, peeled and sliced thinly
2 baby carrots, julienne sliced
1 small celeriac, julienne sliced
1 tablespoon dry sherry

FOR SERVING
3–4 spring onions, chopped finely

Slice the duck breast thinly and dust with the seasoned flour. Heat the oil in a wok and throw in the garlic, ginger root, carrots and celeriac. Stir-fry for 2 minutes. Add the duck and stir-fry for another 2 minutes. Pour in the dry sherry and continue to stir-fry for another minute.

Serve on a platter, sprinkled with the spring onions and surrounded by the brown rice pilaf.

Brown Rice Pilaf

5 oz (150 g) brown rice
2 tablespoons olive oil
1 onion, chopped finely
2 red peppers, cored, seeded and chopped
handful of parsley, chopped finely
sea salt and freshly ground black pepper

Boil the rice for 45 minutes or until tender. Drain well. Meanwhile, heat the oil in a pan and throw in the onion and red peppers. Sauté until just tender. Stir into the rice and add the parsley and seasoning.

Honeyed Tofu

1 packet tofu (morinaga)
3 tablespoons honey
3 fl oz (90 ml) Beaumes de Venise
3 tablespoons toasted almonds

Drain the tofu, then blend to a smooth purée with the honey and Beaumes de Venise. Place in a dish and sprinkle with the almonds. Chill before serving.

Thursday

BREAKFAST

Fresh fruit juice

Wholemeal toast

Herb tea

LUNCH

Stir-fried shrimp and prawn salad

Wholemeal bread (page 22)

DINNER

Pumpkin soup

•

Cauliflower and chick pea pie

Runner beans in saffron garlic sauce

•

Tomato and basil salad

•

Cheese and fresh fruit

Stir-fried Shrimp and Prawn Salad

2 pints (1.2 litres) prawns
1 tablespoon sesame oil
2 tablespoons pickled ginger (*page 168*)
1 pint (600 ml) shrimps
2 tablespoons soy sauce (shoyu) (*page 168*)
red lettuce leaves
½ bunch of spring onions, chopped finely

Peel the prawns. Heat the sesame oil in a wok with the pickled ginger. Throw in the prawns and the shrimps. Toss them for a minute or two, then add the soy sauce and cook for another minute.

Arrange the red lettuce leaves on a platter. Pile the shellfish in the centre and scatter the chopped spring onions over the lot.

Pumpkin Soup

2 lb (1 kg) pumpkin flesh
2 oz (50 g) butter
sea salt and freshly ground black pepper
pinch of nutmeg
pinch of ginger
2½ pints (1.5 litres) vegetable stock

Dice the pumpkin flesh and discard all the seeds and rind. Melt the butter in a pan and throw in the pumpkin flesh with the seasoning and spices. Cook for a few minutes, then add the vegetable stock. Bring to the boil and simmer for 10 minutes. Allow to cool, then blend to a thin purée. Reheat gently.

Cauliflower and Chick Pea Pie

3 oz (75 g) chick peas, soaked overnight
8 oz (250 g) wholemeal pastry (*page 28*)
1 oz (25 g) butter
1 onion, sliced finely
½ teaspoon cumin seeds
¼ pint (150 ml) water
2 tablespoons soy sauce (shoyu) (*page 168*)
1 tablespoon whole grain mustard such as moutarde de Meaux
sea salt and freshly ground black pepper
1 cauliflower, broken into florets
1 egg, beaten, for glazing

Boil the chick peas in fresh water until tender, about 1½ hours. Drain, reserving ¼ pint (150 ml) of the cooking water. Butter and line a pie dish with two-thirds of the pastry and bake it blind (*see page 28*).

Heat the butter and cook the onion with the cumin until soft. Take half of the chick peas and blend them with the water, shoyu, mustard, cooked onions and seasoning. Boil the cauliflower florets until just tender, about 4 minutes. Drain well.

Arrange the florets in the pie dish and fill the spaces between with the whole chick peas. Pour over the blended chick pea mixture. Roll out the rest of the pastry to fit the top of the pie and brush with the beaten egg to glaze. Bake in a preheated oven, 375°F/190°C/gas 5, for 45 minutes (protecting the top for the first 30 minutes).

Runner Beans in Saffron Garlic Sauce

1 head of garlic
2 tablespoons olive oil
½ teaspoon saffron strands
8 fl oz (250 ml) water
sea salt and freshly ground black pepper
2 lb (1 kg) runner beans.

Peel the cloves from the head of garlic. Heat the oil in a pan and sweat the cloves in the oil for a moment or two. Add the saffron, water and seasoning, bring to the boil and simmer for 30 minutes. Leave to cool and then blend.

Meanwhile, trim and slice the beans into chunks (not absurd strands) and boil or steam until just tender. Pour into a serving dish, reheat the sauce and pour over the beans.

Tomato and Basil Salad

1½ lb (750 g) tomatoes
1 tablespoon lemon juice
3 tablespoons olive oil
sea salt and freshly ground black pepper
bunch of basil leaves

Slice the tomatoes and lay them in a shallow dish. Mix the lemon juice, oil and seasoning together and dribble over the tomatoes. Coarsely chop the basil leaves and scatter over the tomatoes.

Friday

BREAKFAST

Pink grapefruit

Herb tea

LUNCH

Mushroom soup

Wholemeal bread (page 22)

DINNER

Pepperoni in tortiera

•

Indonesian fish steaks

Bulgur wheat pilaf

•

Leaf salad

•

Cheese and fresh fruit

Mushroom Soup

1 thick slice of bread
2 pints (1.2 litres) vegetable stock
1 lb (500 g) mushrooms
3 oz (75 g) butter
2 cloves of garlic, crushed
pinch of nutmeg
sea salt and freshly ground black pepper
handful of parsley, chopped
¼ pint (150 ml) single cream or yoghurt

Place the slice of bread in a shallow bowl and pour a little of the cold stock over it.

Slice the mushrooms thinly with their stalks. Sauté them in the butter with the garlic, nutmeg, seasoning and half the parsley. Leave the pan over a low heat for several minutes with the lid on, and the mushrooms will soften in their own juices. Add the bread, stirring it in so that it disintegrates. Add the remaining stock and cook for a further 5 minutes.

Leave to cool, then blend. The soup should have a thin consistency. Reheat, and add the cream or yoghurt and the rest of the parsley.

Pepperoni in Tortiera

1 green, 1 yellow and 1 red pepper
3 cloves of garlic, crushed
1 tablespoon each of chopped mint and parsley
3 tablespoons wholemeal breadcrumbs
5 tablespoons olive oil
1 tablespoon lemon juice
sea salt and freshly ground black pepper
6 black olives, stoned and sliced

Burn and blister the peppers under a hot grill or over a flame. Scrape the skins away. Slice the flesh into strips and discard the cores and seeds. Lay the strips in a shallow dish.

Add the crushed garlic and herbs to the breadcrumbs with 2 tablespoons of the oil, then add the lemon juice and seasoning. Pour this over the peppers. Scatter the chopped olives over the top. Pour over the rest of the oil and bake in a preheated oven, 400°F/200°C/gas 6, for about 10–12 minutes. Serve hot or warm.

Indonesian Fish Steaks

1½ lb (750 g) white fish (shark, monkfish, rock salmon, halibut, cod
or haddock), cut into 4–6 steaks
2 tablespoons olive oil
4 cloves of garlic, sliced
1 dried red chilli, crushed
½ teaspoon each of fenugreek, ground turmeric and mustard seeds
1 lb (500 g) sweet potatoes, diced small
2 tablespoons white wine
2 tablespoons water
sea salt and freshly ground black pepper

Prepare the steaks by trimming the skin and bone from them.

Heat the olive oil and sweat the garlic, chilli, fenugreek, turmeric and mustard seeds. Throw in the sweet potato and cook over low heat for a few minutes. Then add the wine, water and seasoning. Cook for 10 minutes by which time the sweet potato should have become a chunky purée.

Pour into an oven dish and arrange the steaks on top. Cook in a preheated oven, 375°F/190°C/gas 5, for 15 minutes.

Bulgur Wheat Pilaf

5 oz (150 g) bulgur wheat
1 lb (500 g) French beans
1 bunch of spring onions, chopped finely
1 oz (25 g) butter
sea salt and freshly ground black pepper

Place the bulgur wheat in a bowl and pour boiling water over it, just to cover. Leave for 30 minutes by which time it will have absorbed all the liquid. Meanwhile, trim and chop the beans and briefly steam or boil them until just tender. Add to the bulgur wheat with the spring onions.

Melt the butter in a pan and throw in the pilaf with some seasoning. Quickly sauté so that it is heated through and then serve.

Saturday

BREAKFAST

Fresh fruit juice

Wholemeal toast

LUNCH

Simple fish soup

Wholemeal bread (page 22)

DINNER PARTY

Globe artichokes stuffed with Brussels sprout purée

•

Roast pheasant with quinces

Roast potatoes

Glazed beetroot

Spinach

•

Tunstall apple tart

Simple Fish Soup

1 lb (500 g) mixed white fish, with bones and heads
1 bouquet garni
1 onion, chopped finely
1 bay leaf
juice and peel of 1 lemon
2 pints (1.2 litres) water
sea salt and freshly ground black pepper
¼ pint (150 ml) white wine
generous handful of parsley, chopped finely

Place everything except the wine and parsley in a large pan. Bring to the boil and simmer for 20 minutes. Leave to cool, drain (reserving the liquor), then take the fish flesh from the bones and flake. Discard the bones with the bay leaf, bouquet garni and lemon peel.

Put the flaked flesh back into the pan with the liquor. Bring to the boil and pour in the white wine. Cook for a few more minutes, then add the parsley before serving.

Garlic croûtons (*page 129*) and rouille go excellently with this soup.

Rouille

2 egg yolks
1 teaspoon powdered mustard
1 teaspoon chilli powder
½ pint (300 ml) olive oil
1 tablespoon tomato purée
1 tablespoon lemon juice
sea salt

Mix the yolks with the mustard powder and chilli powder to a stiff paste in a bowl, then add the oil drop by drop to make an emulsion. When all the oil is absorbed, beat in the tomato purée and lemon juice. Add sea salt to taste. This makes a fairly hot rouille; use ½ teaspoon chilli powder for a less hot sauce.

Globe Artichokes stuffed with Brussels Sprout Purée

4–6 large globe artichokes
1 lb (500 g) Brussels sprouts
1 oz (25 g) butter
2 oz (50 g) curd cheese
sea salt and freshly ground black pepper

Remove artichoke stalk and trim the points of the leaves. Boil the artichokes for 45 minutes, then let them drain and cool. Extract the centre leaves with the choke (use a sharp pointed spoon), leaving a surround of the large leaves with the artichoke bottom exposed.

Trim and boil the sprouts until tender. Drain and place in a blender with the butter, curd cheese and seasoning. Blend to a thick purée. Place about 2 tablespoons of the purée into each artichoke and serve.

Roast Pheasant with Quinces

brace of dressed pheasants
2 sprigs of rosemary
1 tablespoon olive oil
juice and zest of 3 oranges
sea salt and freshly ground black pepper
5–6 quinces

Stuff the pheasants with the sprigs of rosemary and place in a roasting bag with the olive oil, orange juice and zest, and seasoning. Peel the quinces, slice them in half and core them. Place them around the pheasants. Protect the breasts with buttered paper, then close the roasting bag but do not puncture it. (Pheasants dry out easily; this method steams them as they roast.)

Cook in a preheated oven, 425°F/220°C/gas 7, for 1¼ hours. Remove from the oven, undo the roasting bag and take off the buttered paper. Return to the oven for another 15 minutes.

Remove the rosemary and serve the pheasant with the quinces and the juices in the pan.

Glazed Beetroot

8–10 small beetroots
2 tablespoons honey

Trim the beetroot, then boil them for 1½ hours or until tender. Leave to cool and then skin them.

Put the honey in an oven dish and heat it. Throw in the beetroot and toss in the honey. Bake in a hot oven, 425°F/220°C/gas 7, for 10 minutes.

Tunstall Apple Tart

FOR THE PASTRY
8 oz (250 g) white flour
1 tablespoon icing sugar
salt
5 oz (150 g) butter, iced and grated
1 egg yolk
2–3 tablespoons iced water

FOR THE FILLING
1 lb (500 g) cooking apples
1 oz (25 g) butter
1 lb (500 g) dessert apples
2 tablespoons caster sugar

FOR THE GLAZE
1 tablespoon rum or brandy
3 tablespoons quince, apple or blackcurrant jelly

Make the pastry. Sift the flour, adding the icing sugar and a pinch of salt. Mix in the butter until it resembles fine breadcrumbs. Stir in the egg yolk and enough water to make a paste. Cover in clingfilm and refrigerate for 1 hour. Bring back to room temperature and roll out to line a 11 × 1 in (28 × 2.5 cm) tart tin. Bake blind (see page 28).

Peel and core the cooking apples. Place in a pan with the butter over low heat. Cook until they have gone into a purée. Fill the bottom of the pastry shell with the purée. Peel and slice the dessert apples and arrange over the apple purée in a fan shape. Sprinkle with the sugar and grill under a preheated grill for 3–5 minutes, making sure the apples are done evenly. To make the glaze, heat the rum or brandy, add the fruit jelly, stir until it melts and pour over the tart. Leave until well cooled.

Sunday

BRUNCH

Stuffed pancakes

Cheese muffins

Roulade of smoked fish

Carrots in damson purée

Pasta and nut salad

Apple and blackberry fool

Sparkling wine and fruit juice

SUPPER

Pheasant pilaf

Pancakes stuffed with Avocado and Onion

FOR THE PANCAKES
4 oz (125 g) plain flour
4 oz (125 g) wholemeal flour
½ teaspoon salt
2 eggs
½ pint (300 ml) skimmed milk
½ pint (300 ml) water

FOR THE STUFFING
3 ripe avocados, peeled and stoned
1 bunch of spring onions, chopped
1 large onion, peeled and sliced finely
1 tablespoon green peppercorns
5 oz (150 g) curd cheese
juice and zest of 1 lemon

Sift the flours into a mixing bowl and pour back the bran from the sieve. Add the salt. Make a well in the centre, and break in the eggs. Mix the eggs into the flour so that there is a thick paste. Combine the milk and water and add to the mixture, a little at a time, whisking until all the liquid is absorbed and you have a thin batter. Continue to whisk for a few minutes so that the batter is bubbly.

Leave to rest for 1 hour before use. Mix all the stuffing ingredients together thoroughly. Whisk the batter immediately before making pancakes in the usual manner. This batter will make 8 pancakes. Stuff with the avocado and onion mixture.

Cheese Muffins

5 oz (150 g) maize flour or cornmeal
3 oz (75 g) wholemeal flour
1 tablespoon baking powder
4 oz (125 g) matured Cheddar, grated
1 tablespoon brown sugar
1 teaspoon sea salt
1 egg
8 fl oz (250 ml) skimmed milk
3 tablespoons corn oil
2 tablespoons sesame seeds

Sift the flours together with the baking powder, mix in grated cheese, sugar and salt. Break in the egg and add the milk and oil. Beat thoroughly using a whisk or an electric beater to make a batter.

Grease a bun tray and pour the batter into each space. Sprinkle with the sesame seeds and bake in a preheated oven, 425°F/220°C/gas 7, for 20 minutes or until the muffins have risen and are brown. Tip them out of the tray onto a wire rack to cool.

Roulade of Smoked Fish

1 smoked trout
4 oz (125 g) smoked salmon, chopped (off-cuts will do)
4 oz (125 g) peeled prawns
juice and zest of 1 lemon
6 oz (175 g) curd cheese or ricotta
generous handful of parsley, chopped finely
sea salt and freshly ground black pepper
8 oz (250 g) puff pastry (thawed if frozen)
1 egg, beaten
1 tablespoon sesame seeds

Skin and bone the trout. Flake the flesh into a bowl, and add the chopped smoked salmon, prawns, lemon juice and zest, cheese, parsley and seasoning. Mix roughly.

Roll out the pastry to about 12 in (30 cm) square. Spread the smoked fish mixture over it, leaving a 1 in (2.5 cm) border all round. Roll up with care. Lift onto a greased baking sheet with the open end underneath, paint with beaten egg and sprinkle with sesame seeds.

Bake in a preheated oven, 400°F/200°C/gas 6, for 30 minutes or until golden brown and puffed up. Leave to cool.

Carrots in Damson Purée

2 lb (1 kg) baby carrots
8 oz (250 g) damsons
3 fl oz (90 ml) dry sherry

Trim and slice the carrots lengthways. Steam them until just tender. Meanwhile, add the sherry to the damsons and stew gently for 5 minutes. Leave to cool, then stone and place in a blender. Purée until smooth. Reheat the purée and dribble over the cooked carrots. Serve at once.

Pasta and Nut Salad

4 oz (125 g) pasta shells (in various colours)
4 tablespoons olive oil
1 tablespoon red wine vinegar
1 tablespoon whole grain mustard such as moutarde de Meaux
2 cloves of garlic, crushed
sea salt and freshly ground black pepper
1 oz (25 g) each of broken walnuts, hazelnuts and almonds
1 savoy cabbage, sliced finely
2 onions, sliced finely
2 cooking apples, grated

Boil the pasta shells in salted water until al dente. Drain well. Mix the oil, vinegar, mustard, garlic and seasoning together to make a vinaigrette. In a large bowl, combine the pasta with all the remaining ingredients and toss well in the vinaigrette.

Apple and Blackberry Fool

2 lb (1 kg) cooking apples
1 lb (500 g) blackberries
½ pint (300 ml) smetana or sour cream
2 egg whites

Peel and core the apples. Place them in a pan with the blackberries and cook until soft, a few minutes. When cool, beat in the smetana. Whip the egg whites until stiff and fold into the mixture. Refrigerate until serving.

Pheasant Pilaf

A delicious game pilaf can easily be made by chopping up the remains of a bird, then using any of the buckwheat, couscous or millet recipes (*pages 73, 42, 67*) and cooking the flesh with the grain adding, perhaps, a little white wine and substituting stock made from the carcass of the bird for the water.

A WORKING PERSON'S GUIDE TO AUTUMN

Busy people do not bother much with first courses, although nibbling something while cooking is probably common. Autumn has two vegetables – corn and globe artichokes – that are so good that I have included them as dishes on their own. Corn on the cob can be cooked in 8 minutes; globe artichokes need, depending on size, anything from 30 to 45 minutes but several can be cooked at the same time and kept in the refrigerator to be eaten when you want to. Corn should be eaten with a little butter and lots of black pepper. Artichokes are best with a strong garlic vinaigrette.

Fresh fish, simply grilled, is always good, easy food. I have given some suggestions for cooking fish in the introduction to the summer season (*see page 97*), but I cannot resist giving a recipe here for skate in black butter and capers, for it is a classic dish and takes under 10 minutes to cook.

Quail are the only game to appear here, but in this recipe are simple to prepare and quick to cook.

Dinner

MONDAY

Corn on the cob

Pasta shapes with courgettes

Green salad

Fruit

TUESDAY

Prawn roulade

Lettuce Clamart

Fruit and cheese

WEDNESDAY

Skate in black butter

Potato purée (page 35)

Fruit and cheese

THURSDAY

Globe artichokes

Mushroom turnover

Fruit and cheese

FRIDAY

Sautéed quail

Grain pilaf (page 120)

Courgette and basil salad

Fruit and cheese

MONDAY

Pasta Shapes with Courgettes

4 oz (125 g) pasta shapes
3 tablespoons olive oil
2 cloves of garlic, crushed
8 oz (250 g) courgettes, sliced
1 oz (25 g) butter
2 tablespoons chopped parsley
sea salt and freshly ground black pepper
1–2 tablespoons freshly grated Parmesan

Boil the pasta for about 5 minutes until it is al dente. Meanwhile, heat the olive oil in a pan with the garlic and throw in the courgettes. Sauté them for about 10 minutes.

Drain the pasta and toss in the butter. Add the courgettes, parsley and seasoning. Sprinkle the Parmesan over and serve.

TUESDAY

Prawn Roulade

1 small packet of frozen puff pastry, thawed
8 oz (250 g) frozen prawns, thawed and drained
½ bunch of spring onions, chopped
5 oz (175 g) curd cheese
sea salt and freshly ground black pepper
1 egg, beaten

Roll out the puff pastry to a rectangle. Mix the prawns with the spring onions, curd cheese and seasoning. Use half of the beaten egg to moisten the mixture. Spread it over the pastry, leaving a ½ in (1 cm) border.

Roll up the pastry carefully lengthways and place on a greased baking tray with the open end underneath. Glaze with the rest of the beaten egg and bake in a preheated oven, 425°F/220°C/gas 7, for 30 minutes or until puffed up and golden brown.

Lettuce Clamart

1½ lb (750 g) fresh garden peas
1 cos lettuce
4 or 5 shallots
2 oz (50 g) butter
¼ pint (150 ml) dry white wine
sea salt and freshly ground black pepper

Pod the peas and tear the leaves from the lettuce. Chop the shallots finely. Melt the butter in a large pan and add the shallots and lettuce leaves. Let them cook in the butter and their own juices for a couple of minutes, then add the peas, wine and seasoning. Lower the heat. Place a tightly fitting lid on the pan and cook for 10–12 minutes.

WEDNESDAY

Skate in Black Butter

plain flour
8 oz (250 g) skate wing
2 oz (50 g) butter
2 tablespoons capers
2 tablespoons wine vinegar

Lightly flour the skate. Melt the butter in a pan and fry the fish on both sides until it is done, about 3 minutes for each side. Take the fish out and keep warm. Add the capers and wine vinegar and deglaze the pan, making a thin bubbling sauce. Pour over the fish and serve.

A potato purée is excellent with this dish. I would be tempted to eat runner beans as a side dish, or fresh peas or mange-touts if there were any around.

Mushroom Turnover

4 oz (125 g) mushrooms, sliced
1 oz (25 g) butter
2 oz (50 g) curd cheese
2 oz (50 g) matured Cheddar, grated
2 tablespoons chopped parsley
sea salt and freshly ground black pepper
1 small packet of shortcrust pastry
1 egg, beaten

Cook the mushrooms in the butter until just soft. Mix them with the curd cheese, Cheddar, parsley and seasoning. Roll out the pastry into a square. Spoon the mixture over one half, leaving a border of ½ in (1 cm). Paint the border with some of the beaten egg, fold over the pastry and press the ends down. Glaze with the rest of the egg.

Bake in a preheated oven, 425°F/220°C/gas 7, for 20–25 minutes or until golden brown.

FRIDAY

Sautéed Quail

2 quail
seasoned flour
1 oz (25 g) butter
2 tablespoons olive oil
3 cloves of garlic, crushed
1 teaspoon oregano
3 fl oz (75 ml) red wine

Cut the quail in half and flatten them with a mallet. Sprinkle seasoned flour over them. Melt the butter and olive oil in a pan, add the garlic and oregano and the quail. Cook first on the outside, then turn them over and cook the other side, allowing 3 minutes for each side. Pour in the red wine and deglaze the pan. Take out the quail and pour the sauce over them.

Eat with one of the grain pilafs (*see pages 67, 120, 144*).

Courgette and Basil Salad

3 or 4 baby courgettes
sea salt
handful of basil leaves, roughly chopped
1 tablespoon walnut oil
1 teaspoon lemon juice
freshly ground black pepper

Grate the courgettes into a colander. Sprinkle with a little sea salt and leave for half an hour. Press some of the liquid from them and then put them into a salad bowl, adding the rest of the ingredients. Toss thoroughly.

GLOSSARY

Cassia is the dried bark of a tree which gives us cinnamon. This is also the bark but planed thin and powdered. Cassia is more pungent than cinnamon and easier to use in cooking than a cinnamon stick which tends to break.

Gram flour, also called besan, is the ground flour from chick peas. It is high in protein and has a pleasant, slightly nutty flavour. Marvellous for thickening curries, stews and soups, it also makes a good batter and is the flour used in pakoras and bhajias. It needs to be sieved to remove lumps before using.

Ginger, pickled is sold in packets under the name of sushi ginger and can be stored after opening in the refrigerator for a couple of weeks. Marvellous for adding to stir-fried vegetables with or without fish, or as an edible garnish, or in salads.

Kuzu flour comes from the powdered kuzu root and will thicken like cornflour or arrowroot but, unlike these others, kuzu is high in protein. It can be bought in packets in wholefood shops.

Quark is a low fat, skimmed milk, soft cheese with only 5% of milk fat, though the most popular variety has only 1% of fat in it. Useful as a substitute for cream in cooking or it can be used as part of a dessert with fresh fruit.

Smetana, a low fat, sour cream, available now from many supermarkets. Higher in fat than quark, but excellent for using as a cream substitute or instead of sour cream, say in borscht.

Shoyu is soy sauce of high quality made from fermented soy beans and salt. It is worth paying the higher price for this soy as the flavour much improves dishes to which it is added. Cheaper soy sauce is often made only from chemicals and has never seen a soy bean. Shoyu, because it is based on the soy bean, also has protein value.

Tamarind comes from the tamarind tree and is the pulp around the seeds. It contains tartaric acid and has a strong, fruity, lemony taste which is quite delicious. Excellent in curries and sauces with fish, it goes very well too with game to boost a wine sauce. Pour a little boiling water over a tablespoon of tamarind (it appears like a dark sticky goo) and once soft, mix to a purée. Then it can be dissolved in a sauce.

Wasabi powder, or Japanese horseradish, is sold in powdered form in small tins. It is the tiny green cone on the plate served with the food in Japanese restaurants. It is very hot indeed. Mix it with water and leave for 15 minutes.

Vecon is a natural vegetable stock. It comes in jars looking like yeast extracts, but it is hydrolysed vegetable protein, high in vitamins and minerals. I think it is delicious and use it as a spread on toast or in sandwiches. Useful for adding flavour to soups and stews but take care it does not swamp other more delicate flavours.

INDEX

A

Almond and leek soup, 69
Apple, and blackberry fool, 160
   and cabbage salad, 29
   and celery salad, 69
   juice, 142
   tart, Tunstall, 155
Apricot, fool, 47
   tofu, 76
Artichokes, globe, 133, 161
   stuffed with Brussels sprout
      purée, 154
Asparagus, and broad bean stuffed
      pancakes, 100
   filo pie, 82
Aubergine, smoked, to stuff peppers,
   109
Austrian red cabbage, 136
Avocado, and lemon soup, chilled,
   103
   omelette, 129
   and onion stuffed pancakes, 157
   papaya and smoked tofu salad, 45
   soup, hot, 27
   and spinach salad, 91

B

Baked glazed pineapple, 82
Baked spiced potatoes, 140
Basil, and courgette salad, 166
   and tomato salad, 148
Beans, dried
   baked, home-made, 51
   and cabbage salad, 54
   and nut salad, 72
   and spinach tart, quick, 56
   black, and ginger soup, 35
   black, in millet pilaf with ginger, 36
   black-eyed, and endive salad, 137
   haricot, soup, 66
   mung dhal, 24
   mung soup, 26
   salad, mixed, 75

spiced croûte, 92
Beans, fresh
   broad, in parsley sauce, 92
   broad, tomato and onion salad,
      109
   broad, pancakes stuffed with, 127
   broad, pancakes stuffed with
      asparagus and, 100
   French, with millet pilaf, 93
   runner, in saffron garlic sauce,
      147
Beetroot, and chilli soup, 135
   glazed, 155
Besan, 168
Black beans
   and ginger soup, 35
   in millet pilaf, 36
Blackberry and apple fool, 160
Black-eyed beans
   and endive salad, 137
   salad, mixed, 75
   and spinach tart, quick, 56
Braised fennel, 79
Bread, 17
   garlic, 127
   herb granary loaf, 40
   high protein loaf, 26
   pitta, stuffed, 49
   stuffed, 84
   wholemeal, 22
Breakfast, 17
Brioche, cheese, 49
Broad beans
   in parsley sauce, 92
   pancakes, stuffed with, 127
   pancakes stuffed with asparagus
      and, 100
   tomato and onion salad, 109
Broccoli and macaroni cheese, 110
Brown rice pilaf, 144
Brussels sprout purée, to stuff globe
      artichokes, 154
Buckwheat and carrot croquettes, 73
Bulgur wheat pilaf, 151

C

Cabbage, and apple salad, 29
and bean salad, 54
leaves for walnut and onion
moulds, 22
and pea soup, 31
red, Austrian, 136
rolls, 76
Cannelloni stuffed with mushrooms
and laver, 113
Caper sauce, hot, 32
Carrot and buckwheat croquettes, 73
Carrots in damson purée, 159
Casserole, simple pigeon, 45
vegetable, 36
Cassia, 168
Cauliflower, cheese, 87
and chick pea pie, 147
Celeriac, steamed, salad, 42
Celery and apple salad, 69
Cereal, marinated, 39, 63, 65, 142
Cheese, 19
brioche, 49
cauliflower, 87
cottage, and cucumber salad, 103
feta, fresh pea and tomato salad,
112
goat's, savoury, 47
haloumi, 88
light blue sauce with spinach
mould, 41
macaroni and broccoli, 110
muffins, 158
Cherry, melon and lychee salad, 86
Chick pea, and cauliflower pie, 147
and pasta salad, 119
Chick peas with garlic croûtons, 129
Chicory, and orange salad, 24
grapefruit and walnut salad, 58
Chilled avocado and lemon soup, 103
Chilli and beetroot soup, 135
Chinese leaf salad, 37
Chocolate cream, 29
Cod steaks in orange sauce, 32
Cold vegetable curry, 119
Compote, dried fruit, 44
Cottage cheese and cucumber salad,
103
Courgette and basil salad, 166
Courgettes, pasta shapes with, 163

stir-fried, 73
Couscous, 42
pilaf with grilled scallops, 91
Crab pâté, 99
Croûtons, garlic, 129
Crudités, 121
Cucumber, and cottage cheese salad,
103
salad, 117
Cumin with hummus, 81
Curry, cold vegetable, 119
fish, potato and mushroom, 23

D

Damson purée with carrots, 159
Dhal, green lentil, 57
mung bean, 24
Dried fruit compote, 44
Duck breasts, stir-fried, 143

E

Eggs, 97, 124
avocado omelette, 129
free-range, 11
scrambled, with herbs, 115
Endive and black-eyed bean salad,
137
Exotic fruit salad, 50

F

Falafels of split pea, 32
Fats, 10
Fennel, braised, 79
poached, 104
tomato and watercress salad, 106
Feta, fresh pea and tomato salad, 112
Fibre, 11
Fish, 52
cod steaks in orange sauce, 32
Dover sole, 124
kedgeree, 103
kipper pâté, 112
monkfish kebab, 93
pie, 79
potato and mushroom curry, 23
roulade of smoked, 158
salmon, 97
salmon, marinated, 128